Beyond Human Rights

BEYOND HUMAN RIGHTS

DEFENDING FREEDOMS

Alain de Benoist

Foreword by Eric Maulin,
Professor of Public Law at Strasbourg University
& Director of the Institut des Hautes Études Européennes

ARKTOS
MMXI

First English edition published in 2011 by Arktos Media Ltd., originally published as *Au-delà des droits de l'homme: Pour défendre les libertés* (Paris: Krisis, 2004).

© 2011 Arktos Media Ltd.

Printed in the United Kingdom

ISBN 978-1-907166-20-4

BIC classification: Social & political philosophy (HPS)
Human rights (JPVH)

Translator: Dr Alexander Jacob
Editor: John B. Morgan
Cover Design: Andreas Nilsson
Layout: Daniel Friberg
Proofreader: Matthew Peters

ARKTOS MEDIA LTD

www.arktos.com

TABLE OF CONTENTS

A NOTE FROM THE EDITOR

Unless otherwise indicated, the footnotes to the text were added by the author himself for the original French edition. Additional footnotes which were added by me are so marked. Where sources in other languages have been cited, I have attempted to replace them with existing English-language editions. Citations to works for which I could locate no translation are retained in their original language. Web site addresses for on-line sources were verified as accurate and available during May and June 2011.

I would like to thank Prof. Eric Maulin, who kindly contributed an original Foreword for this volume on extremely short notice. I would also like to extend my appreciation to Sergio Knipe, who translated the Foreword; to Dr. Alexander Jacob, who made some clarifications regarding the translation of the Foreword; and to Matthew Peters, for his extraordinary contributions as a proofreader.

-JOHN B. MORGAN IV

FOREWORD

Summum ius, summa injuria.[1] There is, perhaps, no other area of law where Cicero's saying (well-known to all lovers of dictionaries of quotations) is more applicable than human rights. In the name of humanity, the Empire of Good will bomb Belgrade, Baghdad or Tripoli, foment colour revolutions in former Soviet states, set the Maghreb and the Near East ablaze, and seek to universally impose its fundamentalist conception of democracy. Squads of businessmen dispatched by corporations will follow the ideological bulldozers driven by the evangelists. How many times have popular revolutions been hijacked by social benefactors chiefly interested in serving the interests of the people behind them?

Already in the late 1970s — with the onset of the second wave of globalisation — the philosopher Marcel Gauchet observed how the defence of human rights had been turned into a substitution policy.[2] This metamorphosis has continued: from politics, one has moved on to religion, so much so that today — as Alain de Benoist observes in the present volume — 'it is as unseemly, blasphemous and shocking to criticise the ideology of human rights as it once was to doubt the existence of God'. In this context, works critical of human rights — meaning works written in a critical spirit — can only be beneficial. With the eyes of a lynx, at the beginning of this transformation, Michel Villey had set

---

1 Latin: 'the extreme law is the greatest injustice'. From Cicero, 'On Duties', book one, chapter 33.-Ed.

2 Marcel Gauchet, 'Les droits de l'homme ne sont pas une politique', in Le Débat, no. 3, July-August 1980, pp. 2-21; reprinted in La démocratie contre elle-même (Paris: Gallimard, 2002).

out precisely to provide such a critique.[3] He caused quite a bit of con-
sternation and his work is now read neither in law faculties nor anywhere else. Is Alain de Benoist's work destined to meet the same fate?
We bet it won't. Still, the sanctimonious are gathered in their palaces:
the Venetian palaces housing the mighty Venice Commission. These
constitutional engineers are developing principles of political justice to
be adopted by all states seeking admission into one of the many European organisations, starting from the European Council and European
Union. In the Palace of Nations in Geneva, away from the cries of the
people, experts are setting down universally applicable human rights
laws and the ways in which these are to be applied. In the Palace of
the Rights of Man,[4] in Strasbourg, great inscrutable judges, enveloped
in long silk robes, unflinchingly issue regulatory judgements reversing
previous laws, overruling parliaments and bypassing the constitutions
of sovereign states. It is difficult to make this criticism heard because
the Church of Human Rights is so powerful that it imposes as self-
evident doctrines which rest on nothing but sheer assumptions, and
which often go against the most ancient laws in peoples' traditions.

It is upon these assumptions that Alain de Benoist focuses, inves-
tigating the origins, basis, universality and influence of human rights.
In doing so, he undermines the very foundations of human rights and
their underlying claims.

1. Human rights are often presented as being timeless rights. Take the
Preamble to the *Declaration of the Rights of Man and of the Citizen* of
1789:[5]

> The representatives of the French people, constituted in the National
> Assembly, considering that ignorance, forgetfulness or contempt of
> the rights of man are the only causes of public misfortunes and the
> corruption of governments, have resolved to set forth, in a solemn
> declaration, natural rights, inalienable and sacred to man.

---

3 Michel Villey, *Le Droit et les Droits de l'homme* (Paris: Presses universitaires de
   France [PUF], 1983).

4 Otherwise known as the European Court of Human Rights.-Ed.

5 *The Declaration of the Rights of Man and of the Citizen* was adopted by the French
   Constituent Assembly during the French Revolution, in August 1789.-Ed.

Forgetfulness or contempt, according to this declaratory rhetoric, justifies the need to reinstate rights which nonetheless *already exist.* It is for this reason that the first French Revolutionaries were so keen to draw a distinction between the Declaration of 1789 on the one hand and the Constitution of 1791 on the other. The former reinstates what is already in existence, whereas the latter establishes something which previously did not exist; the former invokes an alleged tradition, the latter forges institutions for the new man. But clearly this is a largely rhetorical distinction. The antiquity of the rights invoked serves to justify the promotion of the new man, *Homo oeconomicus,*[6] whose actions are entirely calculated to match the algorithm of his own interests and whose behaviour can be standardised.

Antiquity, however, ignored the idea of fundamental rights. Neither the Greeks nor the Romans believed there could be such a thing as what we call human rights, which are subjective rights attached to all human individuals as subjects. For human rights to become possible, the notion of the individual had to be invented, and Norbert Elias has shown that there was no equivalent to it in Antiquity.[7] Alain de Benoist stresses the important role which the Christian religion played in the birth of the idea of the individual. This is not to say that individuals did not exist before Christianity (to think so would be absurd); simply, individuals were not acknowledged as such. For the category of the individual to make its appearance — the prerequisite for the birth of human rights — it was necessary to attribute a unique value to each human being, a soul which would connect it to God. Starting from the individual, it then became possible to think in terms of subjects; starting from subjects, in terms of subjective rights; and starting from subjective rights, in terms of human rights. Naturally, this was no linear progression; yet it indicates an axis which ultimately runs from St. Augustine to Locke and Kant. From the Sixteenth century onwards, it has contributed to the development of modern natural law, which has

---

6   Latin: 'economic man'.-Ed.
7   Norbert Elias, *The Society of Individuals* (Oxford: Basil Blackwell, 1991).

found its chief representatives in Grotius,[8] Pufendorf,[9] Locke[10] and Wolff[11] and has exercised a considerable influence upon the thought of both the Founding Fathers of the United States and the French Revolutionaries.[12]

The anthropological revolution which made it possible to think of man as an individual immediately went hand-in-hand with a juridical revolution which imposed the idea that individuals are *equal before the law*, i.e., that they possess inalienable subjective rights. Differences among men thus came to be regarded as something merely contingent, secondary and social, and hence commonly perceived as unjust. So much so that, as René Girard has illustrated, it is equality — through the mimetic rivalry it engenders — and not mutual difference which is the major cause of conflict among men.[13] Alain de Benoist has written that a triple revolution has shaped modernity: 'On the one hand, the notion of will is substituted for the notion of order. On the other hand, the individual has moved to the centre and the law has become his attribute. Finally, the law is identified with "justice", the latter having henceforth an essentially moral complexion.' This triple revolution clearly shows that human rights are far from eternal and that their alleged universality is merely the expression of an ideology, which is to say of a system for representing the world and man's place in the world which has being developing and incessantly changing since late Antiquity. In its modern form, the anthropology of subjects is a

---

8 Hugo Grotius (1583-1645) was a Dutch jurist who is considered one of the founders of international law based upon the principles of natural law, in particular as it pertains to the conditions for the justifications of war.-Ed.

9 Samuel von Pufendorf (1632-1694) was a German political philosopher and statesman. He asserted that the authority of the state depends for its power upon the combined wills of the individuals that comprise it.-Ed.

10 John Locke (1632-1704) was an English philosopher of the Enlightenment who is regarded as the most important theorist of liberalism, as his works were extremely important to the development of modern democracy.-Ed.

11 Christian Wolff (1679-1754) was a German philosopher who viewed human society in the same way as the division between body and soul, in which the soul is the leadership of the state and the body represents its subjects, which comprise the majority of the populace.-Ed.

12 Georg Jellinek, *The Declaration of the Rights of Man and of Citizens: A Contribution to Modern Constitutional History* (Wesport: Hyperion Press, 1979).

13 René Girard, *Violence and the Sacred* (Baltimore: The Johns Hopkins University Press, 1977).

recent invention.[14] It is based on an abstract conception of the individual, reduced to certain constitutive elements whose combinations standardise our actions.

2. Human rights, however, are presented not in terms of their historicity — for this would weaken their authority by relativising them — but through a philosophical tale of their foundations. It is always very important to clearly distinguish the historical question of origins from the philosophical one of foundations. Alain de Benoist must be credited for having drawn a perfect distinction between the two issues.

In its basic version, the question of the foundations of human rights may be formulated starting from social contract theories. Indeed, explanations not of the origins of society but of its foundations were first developed within the school of modern natural law, a current of thought which began with Grotius' publication of the treatise *The Rights of War and Peace*[15] in 1625 and which continued into the Eighteenth century. The various social contract theories vary significantly, to the point they are mutually irreducible. Still, they follow a line of thought that may be summed up as follows: free individuals exist in the state of nature. In order for them to defend their own freedom and property, they soon realised they needed a common power which could secure their fundamental rights. The state, which is to say public power, results from an agreement among free individuals who have regrouped to form an association. The political constitution which serves as a law for them is the contract which brings them together. All the elements behind the theory of human rights are already present in this mythological account: the individual in the state of nature is a *Homo oeconomicus*, a free individual and property owner concerned with defending his own interests. Through rational planning, he reaches the conclusion that the establishment of the state is necessary if he is to defend his own interests. As individuals are essentially rational, a collective choice can only lead to a contract. Case made. The same reasoning may be applied at the level of states to justify the establishment of an international society.

---

14 Regarding this matter, we shall refer to the overview provided by J. B. Schneewind, *The Invention of Autonomy: A History of Modern Moral Philosophy* (Cambridge: Cambridge University Press, 1998).

15 *Grotius on the Rights of War and Peace: An Abridged Translation* (Clark: The Lawbook Exchange, 2009).

This line of reasoning, sprung from Seventeenth-century philosophical treatises, has not yet grown outdated. It is still to be found at the very heart of the most sophisticated contemporary theories. John Rawls' *A Theory of Justice*,[16] which is often regarded as the greatest work of political philosophy of the Twentieth century, is nothing but an elaborate reformulation of social contract theories. Some of the major interpretations of globalisation, such as Francis Fukuyama's theory about the end of history[17] or James Rosenau's idea of *global governance*,[18] are based on the same assumptions. Social contract theory is not an old theory belonging to the history of political philosophy, but rather something which is constantly being updated and expanded, and which serves as a foundation for theories of international law. The recent theory about 'the responsibility to protect' which has been applied by the United Nations Security Council in the Ivory Coast and in Libya ultimately rests on Locke's idea that rulers only derive their legitimacy from the protection they afford the freedom and property of individuals, thus losing all legitimacy the moment they oppose any insurrection in the name of freedom. When the social contract is severed, the NATO air forces will intervene to restore it.

3. The above observations lead us to another question, which is also raised by Alain de Benoist in his work, namely the issue of the universality of human rights. Human rights are spreading globally. Does this mean they are universal? A distinction must clearly be drawn between the two questions. The first is a practical matter, the latter a juridical one. Still, the two questions are interrelated. The idea that human rights are universal will lead people to search for ways of extending their applicability. The just war is the unavoidable consequence of affirming the universality of human rights.

The alleged universality of human rights is bound to run up against the diversity of cultures and values. One civilisation will expose deformed newborns, while another will euthanise the elderly. The Caribs would eat the flesh of their slain enemies in order to assimilate

---

16 John Rawls, *A Theory of Justice* (Cambridge, MA: Belknap Press, 1971).

17 Francis Fukuyama, *The End of History and the Last Man* (New York: Maxwell Macmillan, 1992).

18 James Rosenau, *Turbulence in World Politics: A Theory of Change and Continuity* (Princeton: Princeton University Press, 1990).

their virtues, while the Incas used to sacrifice a Corn Queen in order to sprinkle their fields with fresh blood. Many populations of sub-Saharan Africa practice female circumcision; Jews and Muslims practice male circumcision. Dying for one's country after killing the highest possible number of enemies was still held to be an honour only fifty years ago, while having an abortion was seen as a crime against the nation. Slavery as practiced in ancient Rome and Athens has become the very symbol of degeneration, and yet purchasing a child conceived in the womb of a woman who is renting her uterus is held to be a right in some modern Western countries. A thousand other examples could be cited to illustrate the following point: 'Three degrees of latitude overthrow jurisprudence. A meridian determines the truth. Law has its periods; right has its epochs; Saturn's entry into the house of the Lion marks the origin of a given crime. It is an odd kind of justice to have a river for its boundary. Truth lies on this side of the Pyrenees, error on the other.'[19] Under these conditions, what credibility could the idea of universal human rights have?

A Universal Declaration of Human Rights was adopted through a resolution of the General Assembly of the United Nations on 10 December 1948 in the Palais de Chaillot (yet another palace!), but its applicability remained limited, as is shown by the multiplication of later declarations: the American Declaration of the Rights and Duties of Man, adopted in Bogotá in 1948, the Convention for the Protection of Human Rights and Fundamental Freedoms (known as the European Convention of Human Rights) signed in Strasbourg in 1950, the African Charter on Human and Peoples' Rights adopted in Nairobi in 1981, the Universal Islamic Declaration of Human Rights proclaimed in Paris in 1981, the Arab Charter on Human Rights signed in 1994 and finally adopted in Tunis in 2004, the European Charter on Fundamental Rights adopted in Nice in 2000... Why multiply the declarations if they are all alike? The truth is that, in fact, they are not alike (for some stress rights and others add duties; some contain only fundamental rights, while others also include social or economic rights). Nor do these declarations all stem from the same principles.

---

19 Blaise Pascal, *Pensées and Other Writings* (Oxford: Oxford World's Classics, 1995), § 294, p. 23. Montaigne had already written: 'What truth is it that is bounded by these mountains and that is falsehood in the world beyond them?' in *Apology for Raymond Sebond* (Indianapolis: Hackett, 2003), p. 140.

Take the following example: in its Preamble, the Universal Islamic Declaration of Human Rights contains a resounding statement:

> Therefore we, as Muslims who believe
> a) in God, the Beneficent and Merciful, the Creator, the Sustainer, the Sovereign, the sole Guide of mankind and the Source of all Law;
> b) in the Vicegerency (Khilafah) of man who has been created to fulfil the Will of God on earth;
> c) in the wisdom of Divine guidance brought by the Prophets, whose mission found its culmination in the final Divine message that was conveyed by the Prophet Muhammad (Peace be upon him) to all mankind.[20]

It does not take a great scholar to grasp that the universality referred to here has little to do with the universality of human rights as understood by the European Convention of Human Rights or the European Charter on Fundamental Rights, both of which prudently avoid all references to God and assume man is of one kind.

These few indications are enough to reveal how in the West, in Europe, when talk is made of the universality of human rights, it is real universality — so to speak — which is being referred to, namely that of secularised, individualist societies following a market economy and mass consumption. It is this universality alone which is being offered as a model to the rest of humanity. Besides, it would be easy to show how all the exotic declarations, charters and conventions on human rights are more the product of an incomplete acculturation process, a form of collateral damage caused by the colonisation of consciences, than of any spontaneous drive towards fundamental rights on the part of indigenous elites!

The Western notion of individual rights is far from common to everyone, including those who adopt declarations or charters regarding fundamental rights. As Alain de Benoist well illustrates, the European conception of the individual is simply incomprehensible to most non-Western cultures, which rest on completely different holistic or communitarian foundations.

---

20 Full text available at the Al-Hewar Center Web site (www.alhewar.com/ISLAMDECL.html).-Ed.

4. Much evidence suggests that the spread of human rights is taking an increasingly authoritarian turn. Alain de Benoist begins by focusing on the problem of the emergence of the idea of dignity as a category central to human rights. Ignored in the first declarations from the late Eighteenth century, the dignity of the human person entered the world of human rights after 1945, when it began to be used in the sense of that which distinguishes man — something above the sovereignty of both individuals and peoples. The introduction of the idea of dignity in relation to human rights has led to a substantialist turn. Human rights are not merely subjective but also substantial, meaning they are rights which neither individuals nor peoples can forgo, as they represent the very essence of man.

A fundamentalist conception of human rights has thus emerged which justifies any defence of these rights against the very will of individuals or peoples — defence by means of force.

Through various bodies, the European Council is playing a leading role in spreading this conception. Let us recall here, by way of example, the action of the Venice Commission and of the European Court of Human Rights.

The Venice Commission (officially, the European Commission for Democracy through Law) is an advisory body of the Council of Europe specialising in constitutional matters.[21] It was very active in the 1990s, when it lent advice to the rulers of central and eastern European states by providing them with good constitutional principles. The Commission has played an important role in promoting what is sometimes still referred to as 'democratic conditionality'. Its original aim was to help the former Soviet states to change their constitutions and fundamental laws so that they would be in conformity with European norms by respecting the standards of the European Council — namely, democracy, human rights and the rule of law. Later, the reputation acquired by the Venice Commission enabled it to extend its influence beyond Europe. It is now particularly active in Africa and the Middle East.

Parallel to this, we are witnessing a juridically remarkable development of the European Court of Human Rights, which is going further

---

21 The European Commission for Democracy through Law, better known today as the Venice Commission, was founded in Strasbourg some twenty years ago — on 10 May 1990 — by the 18 member states of the European Council: Austria, Belgium, Cyprus, Denmark, Finland, France, Greece, Ireland, Italy, Luxembourg, Malta, Norway, Portugal, San Marino, Spain, Sweden, Switzerland and Turkey.

and further in its definition of what constitutes real democracy. The Court is setting the main standards for democracy and, in doing so, increasingly affecting the constitutional law of European states, to the point of breaching their independence.[22]

Democracy is literally in the grip of human rights. This form of democracy is called constitutional. Judge Aharon Barak, the former President of the Israeli Supreme Court, summed it up in a rather striking way:

Everyone agrees that a democracy requires the rule of the people, which is usually effectuated through electing representatives in a legislative body. Therefore, frequent elections are necessary to keep these representatives accountable to their constituents… Democracy is not satisfied merely by abiding by proper elections and legislative supremacy. Democracy has its own internal morality based on the dignity and equality of all human beings. Thus, in addition to formal requirements (elections and the rule of the majority), there are also substantive requirements. These are reflected in the supremacy of such underlying democratic values and principles as separation of powers, the rule of law, and independence of the judiciary. They are based on such fundamental values as tolerance, good faith, justice, reasonableness, and public order. Above all, democracy cannot exist without the protection of human rights — rights so essential that they must be insulated from the power of the majority… Democracy is not just the law of rules and legislative supremacy; it is a multidimensional concept. It requires recognition of both the power of the majority and the limitations on that power. It is based on legislative supremacy and on the supremacy of values, principles, and human rights.[23]

This extract from a work by Judge Barak reflects a very common conception of democracy, which is found among several authors: the

---

22 This is a phenomenon which has been studied in detail, yet without any critical spirit, by Florence Jacquemot in *Le standard européen de société démocratique* (Montpellier: Université Montpellier I, 2006), and more recently by Yannick Lécuyer, *L'européanisation des standards démocratique* (Rennes: Presses de l'Université de Rennes, 2011).

23 Aharon Barak, *The Judge in a Democracy* (Princeton: Princeton University Press, 2006), pp. 27-33.

Frenchman Dominique Rousseau,[24] the German Peter Häberle,[25] and the American Stephen Breyer[26] are only some of the zealous defenders of this substantialist conception of democracy, which treats the people chiefly as an ideal and an abstract principle rather than a tangible community brought together by shared values, views and practices.

Alain de Benoist's work offers a particularly enlightening critique of this concept of substantialist or fundamentalist democracy. It will serve as a starting point for thinking *beyond human rights* through a return to political categories. Human rights are not a policy and a policy of human rights is the very negation of politics. Alain de Benoist is fully in line with Carl Schmitt's[27] and Julien Freund's[28] theories about the essence of politics. Indeed, he may be regarded as their real heir.

Eric Maulin,
Professor of Public Law at Strasbourg University
Director of the Institut des Hautes Études Européennes
June 2011

(Translated into English by Sergio Knipe)

---

24 Dominique Rousseau, *Sur le conseil constitutionnel: La doctrine Badinter et la démocratie* (Paris: Descartes & Cie, 1997); Dominique Rousseau (ed.), *La démocratie continue* (Paris: LGDJ, 1995).

25 Peter Häberle, *L'État constitutionnel* (Paris: Economica, 2004).

26 Stephen Breyer, *Active Liberty: Interpreting Our Democratic Constitution*(New York: Alfred A. Knopf, 2006).

27 Carl Schmitt (1888-1985) was an important German jurist who wrote about political science, geopolitics and constitutional law. He was part of the Conservative Revolutionary movement of the Weimar era. He also briefly supported the National Socialists at the beginning of their regime, although they later turned against him. He remains highly influential in the fields of law and philosophy.-Ed.

28 Julien Freund (1921-1993) was a student of Raymond Aron and Carl Schmitt. During the Second World War, he was a member of the French Resistance movement. After the war he became a professor of sociology at the University of Strasbourg. In 1980, in protest against the French educational system and its methods of teaching political science, he decided to retire. He was also a contributor to New Right publications in both Germany and France.-Ed.

INTRODUCTION

One sometimes wonders what Europe has brought to the world, what particularly characterises it. The best reply is perhaps this: the notion of objectivity. Everything else flows from this: the idea of the individual and of the freedom of the individual, the common good insofar as it is distinguished from particular interests, justice as the search for equity (that is to say, the opposite of vengeance), the ethics of science and the respect for empirical data, philosophical thought insofar as it is emancipated from belief and conserves the power of the thinker to think of the world and to question truth by himself, the spirit of restraint and the possibility of self-criticism, the capacity for dialogue, and even the notion of truth.

Universalism is a corruption of objectivity. Whereas objectivity is achieved from particular things, universalism claims to define particularity from an abstract notion posed arbitrarily. Instead of deducing conscience from being, it proceeds in an opposite direction. Universalism does not consist in treating things objectively but from an overarching abstraction from which a knowledge of the nature of things is supposed to follow. It represents the symmetrical opposite of the error of the metaphysics of subjectivity, which reduces the good to that which is good for me or good for us, the true to the judgment of one's own conscience or to the personal. The European tradition has always affirmed man's necessity to struggle against his immediate subjectivity. The entire history of modernity, says Heidegger, is a history of the unravelling of the metaphysics of subjectivity.

Subjectivity leads necessarily to relativism (everything is valid), reaching in this way the egalitarian conclusion of universalism (all are important). Relativism cannot be surmounted except by the arbitration of one's self (or of our selves): my point of view should prevail for the sole reason that it is mine (or that it is ours). The notions of justice and of the common good are destroyed in one blow.

The ideology of human rights combines these two errors. It is universalist insofar as it wishes to impose itself everywhere without consideration for relationships, traditions and contexts. It is subjectivist insofar as it defines rights as the subjective attributes of a single individual.

'The enthronement of human rights', writes Marcel Gauchet, 'is surely the major ideological and political fact of the last twenty years'.[1] Human rights, he adds, have become 'the ideological centre of gravity' of everything that we participate in at present. They are on the verge of replacing, in a hegemonic manner, all sorts of political and social discourses which formerly were articulated from the point of view of notions that are today worn out or discredited (tradition, nation, progress, revolution), as well as of becoming the sole compass of a disoriented epoch, and of supplying a minimal morality to a world in disarray. They are the 'moral horizon of our time', says Robert Badinter.[2] They should become the 'foundation of all societies', adds Kofi Annan.[3] They contain 'in essence the concept of a true world government', declares Jean Daniel.[4]

They are even more than that. Based on propositions declared to be 'evident' ('we hold these truths to be self-evident' can already be found in the American Declaration of Independence of July 1776), they present themselves as a new Ten Commandments. As a new foundation of human order, they seem to have a sacred character. Human rights have thus been able to be defined as the 'creed of humanity' (Nadine

---

1   *La démocratie contre elle-même* (Paris: Gallimard, 2002), p. 326.

2   Robert Badinter (b. 1928) is a lawyer and a long-time politician of the Socialist Party in France who is best-known for his opposition to the death penalty, which was repealed in 1981. De Benoist is referring to Badinter's speech at the 50th anniversary ceremony to mark the signing of the Universal Declaration of Human Rights, which was adopted by the United Nations in 1948. Badinter stated, 'Here is a text which, even more than when it was conceived, marks the moral horizon of our times.'-Ed.

3   Kofi Annan (b. 1938) was Secretary General of the United Nations from 1997 until 2006.-Ed.

4   Jean Daniel (b. 1920) is a French-Jewish journalist and writer known for his liberal humanist positions.-Ed.

Gordimer),[5] and as a 'worldwide secular religion' (Elie Wiesel).[6] They are, writes Régis Debray, 'the last, to date, of our civil religions, the soul of a soulless world'.[7]

One proof of this is its dogmatic character: it cannot be debated. That is why it seems today as unsuitable, as blasphemous, as scandalous to criticise the ideology of human rights as it was earlier to doubt the existence of God. Like every religion, the discussion of human rights seeks to pass off its dogmas as so absolute that one could not discuss them without being extremely stupid, dishonest or wicked. By presenting human rights as 'human' rights, as 'universal' rights, one necessarily withdraws them from criticism — that is to say from the *right* to question them — and, at the same time, one implicitly places their opponents beyond the pale of humanity, since one cannot fight someone who speaks in the name of humanity while remaining human oneself. Finally, just as, the believers once thought they had the duty to convert, by all means, 'infidels' and miscreants, the adherents of the credo of human rights consider themselves as legitimately invested with the mission of imposing these principles on the whole world. Theoretically founded on a principle of tolerance, the ideology of human rights thus reveals itself to be the bearer of the most extreme intolerance, of the most absolute rejection. The Declarations of Rights are not so much declarations of love as declarations of war.

But today the discussion of human rights does not just have as its goal the supply of a substitute ideology after the collapse of the 'grand narratives'. By seeking to impose a particular moral norm on all peoples, it aims at giving the West a good conscience once again

---

5   Nadine Gordimer (b. 1923) is a Jewish South African writer who was known for her involvement in the anti-apartheid movement. She won the Nobel Prize for Literature in 1991. In *The Universal Declaration of Human Rights: Fifty Years and Beyond* (Amityville: Baywood, 1999), p. viii, she wrote that it 'is, and shall remain, the essential document, the touchstone, the creed of humanity that surely sums up all other creeds directing human behavior, if we are to occupy this world together now and in the Twenty-first century'.-Ed.

6   Elie Wiesel (b. 1928) is a Romanian-Jewish Holocaust survivor who is well-known for his books describing the event. In *The Universal Declaration of Human Rights*, p. 3, he wrote, 'The defense of human rights has, in the last fifty years, become a kind of worldwide secular religion'.-Ed.

7   *Que vive la République* (Paris: Odile Jacob, 1989), p. 173. (Jules Régis Debray [b. 1940] is a prominent French Marxist intellectual. He is famous for having been a part of Che Guevara's ill-fated guerrilla insurgency in Bolivia in 1967.-Ed.)

by allowing it to install itself once more as a model and to denounce as 'barbarian' those who refuse this model. In history 'rights' have only too often been that which the masters of the dominant ideology had decided to define in this way. Associated with the expansion of markets, the discussion of human rights constitutes the ideological armour of globalisation. It is above all an instrument of domination, and should be regarded as such.

Men should be able to fight everywhere against tyranny and oppression. To contest the ideology of human rights is thus evidently not to plead for despotism, it is rather to contest that this ideology is the best means of remedying it. It is to question oneself concerning the validity of the foundations of this theory, on the nomological status of these rights, and on the possibilities of manipulation to which they can be subjected. It is thus to propose another solution.

Freedom is a cardinal virtue. It is the very essence of truth. That is why it should be removed from the rut of universalism and subjectivity. That human rights are proclaimed forcefully in an increasingly dehumanised society, where men themselves tend to become objects, and where the commercialisation of social relationships creates everywhere new phenomena of alienation, is probably not an accident. There are many ways of demonstrating respect and solidarity to men. The question of freedoms cannot be resolved in terms of law or of morality. It is above all a political question. It should be resolved politically.

I

ARE HUMAN RIGHTS A PART OF THE LAW?

The ideology of rights classically defines 'human rights' as the innate rights, inherent in human nature, that are borne by every individual since the time of the 'state of nature', that is to say, before the development of all social relations. Being subjective attributes of every man insofar as he is a man, relating to an isolated individual, who is pre-political and pre-social, these rights are therefore necessarily individual in nature: they are those which the individual can implement according to his will alone; they constitute the privileges which the agent that possesses them can enjoy. They are a prerogative of all human beings, supposed to be independent of space and time, valid at all times and in all places independently of personal conditions, political situations and socio-historical attributes, they are besides universal and inalienable by definition. No state can create them, grant or abrogate them, since they pre-date, and are superior to, every social and political form. The public powers can only recognise them by making sure that they guarantee and respect them. The general idea which is deduced from this definition is that man is not reducible to his social being, and that his true self is elsewhere.

Human rights are ahistorical, but they nevertheless have a history. Besides, the expression *jura hominum*[1] besides is not older than 1537.[2] The first question that one should pose consists, therefore, in knowing according to what procedure human rights were able to be recognised

---

1   Latin: 'human rights'.-Ed.
2   The first known use of the expression 'human rights' appeared in the book *Historica Diplomatica Rerum Bataviarum* by Volmerus, which was published in 1537.-Ed.

and then 'declared', and to what extent their legal formulation represents — or does not — a solution that represents a continuity in relation to the traditional forms of the law.

Originally, law was not at all defined as a collection of rules and
norms of conduct (which derive from morality), but as a discipline
aiming at determining the best means of instituting equity within
a relationship. For the Greeks, justice in the legal sense of the term
represented good proportion, the equitable proportion between distributed possessions and duties. The *jus*[3] of Classical Roman law
aimed equally at determining the 'good distribution' that should exist
between men, the just share that should be attributed to everyone:
suum cuique tribuere.[4] Cicero[5] thus says, in relation to civil law, that
'its end is to maintain among citizens, in the distribution of goods and
in legal cases, a just proportion resting on the laws and customs'.[6] The
jurist is one who determines this just distribution. Being constituted
of the equity and rectitude of relationships between persons, justice
aims from that at the harmony of the group. The privileged domain of
the law is therefore that of distributive justice, that is to say, of a justice
placing the citizens in order among themselves and in relation to the
common good. Human nature serves as a reference but is not apprehended according to conscience, independently of all social relations.
It is in itself only an element of a hierarchical Nature which assigns to
it its place and function.

In this conception of Classical natural law, there is no place either
for universalism, or for subjectivism, or for contractualism. A subjective law, a law which would be an attribute of the person outside all
social life, is unthinkable. 'Rights' are only distributions which should
go to such or such, the result of a distribution ordered by the judge.
The law thus never concerns itself with an isolated being, an individual
considered as such. It does not concern itself, either, with man taken in
his generality: generic man remains an empty category. 'The Greeks',
observes Jean-Pierre Vernant, 'are totally deprived of this idea of a sin-
gular individual, the bearer of universal and inalienable rights, which

---

3   Latin: 'justice'.-Ed.

4   Latin: 'to each his own'.-Ed.

5   Marcus Tullius Cicero (106-43 BCE) was a philosopher and famed orator of the
    Roman Republic.-Ed.

6   *De oratore* [On the Orator], Book 1, Chapter 42.

seem to be taken for granted by us[7] — something that did not prevent them from inventing democracy and to honour the notion of freedom more than others.

The first rupture appeared with Christianity. The Christian religion proclaims, in effect, the unique value of every human being by positing him as a value in himself. Insofar as he possesses a soul which puts him in a direct relationship with God, man becomes the bearer of an absolute value, that is to say, of a value which cannot be confused either with his personal qualities or with his belonging to a particular collective group. Concomitantly, Christianity gives a purely individual definition of freedom, which it makes the faculty of choosing, for a person endowed with reason, in accordance with morality, and between the means that lead to an end (*Radix libertatis sicut subjectum est voluntas, sed sicut causa est ratio*,[8] as Thomas Aquinas[9] would say). This accent placed on free will implicitly contains the idea that man can free himself of his natural qualities, that he can effect his choices on the basis of reason alone and thus make the world accord to his will. At the start, this will is posited as a power of consent. The superior life proceeds from a transformation of the will that is the work of grace.

By these major anthropological innovations, Christianity digs a ditch between the origin of man (God) and his temporal existence. It withdraws from the relative existence of the human being the ontological anchoring that is now reserved for the soul. The relations between men are, of course, always important, but they remain secondary, for the simple reason that the common life of men, their collective life, is no longer confused with their being. It is thus not wrongly, from this point of view, that Hegel[10] was able to make the coming of Christianity coincide with subjectivism.

---

7   *Le Monde*, 8 June 1993, p. 2.

8   'The root of liberty is will as the subject thereof; but it is the reason as its cause.' From Thomas Aquinas, *Summa Theologica*: Volume Two, Part Two, First Section (New York: Cosimo, 2007), p. 656.-Ed.

9   St. Thomas Aquinas (1125-1274) was a Dominican priest whose writings became important in both theological and philosophical debates.-Ed.

10 Georg W. F. Hegel (1770-1831) was one of the most important philosophers of the Nineteenth century, being one of the principal founders of the school known as German Idealism.-Ed.

It is above all in the Augustinian[11] tradition that the fact of belonging to the supra-terrestrial city would be affirmed at the expense of that which ties man to those similar to him. 'The Christian ceases to be a *part* of the political organism', writes Michel Villey, 'he is a totality, an infinity, a value in himself. He himself is an end superior to the temporal ends of politics and his person transcends the state. Here is the seed of the modern freedoms of the individual, which will be opposable to the state, our future "human rights"'.[12] By proclaiming the metaphysical destiny of man, Christianity tends to divert human justice from its interest in the world of the senses.

Augustine also develops with force the Christian idea according to which the path towards the higher passes through the interior: *Noli foras ire, in teipsum redi; in interiore homine habitat veritas* ('Do not go abroad. Return within yourself. In the inward man dwells truth').[13] The internal conscience thus replaces the world as the locus of truth. It is through the conscience, the locus of a secret freedom which is also the seat of the soul, that one can go to God. A tendency toward reflexivity is introduced into Western thought through this theme, which will later be transformed into pure subjectivity. The idea that the conscience is the locus of truth announces, in fact, the modern idea of a private sphere, cut off from the public sphere and detached from external contingencies, which would be the privileged place of the blossoming of the individual. Descartes[14] will resume the theme of Augustinian interiority and orient it in a new direction by situating the sources of morality in the *cogito*. Privatisation, one could say; the promotion of

---

11 St. Augustine (354-430) was an important bishop of the latter-day Roman Empire and was one of the Church Fathers. He outlines his idea of the heavenly city in his *City of God.*-Ed.

12 *Philosophie du droit*, vol. 1: *Définitions et fins du droit*, 3rd ed. (Paris: Dalloz, 1982), p. 131.

13 This is from Augustine's *On True Religion*, in *Augustine: Earlier Writings* (Louisville: Westminster John Knox Press, 2006), p. 262.-Ed.

14 René Descartes (1596-1650) was a French philosopher who initiated many of the trends and ideas which have come to preoccupy modern philosophy and science in particular. One of his central efforts was to determine how one can be certain that anything actually exists. His most famous formulation is the proof he offered in his *Meditations on First Philosophy*: *cogito ergo sum*, or 'I think, therefore I am'. Although we can doubt the existence of objects in the world, the fact that we are capable of thinking about them is proof positive that we ourselves exist.-Ed.

a private sphere where the good life is reduced henceforth to the ordinary life, begins with this promotion of the conscience.

The belief in a sole God allows one, besides, to represent all men without distinction as being equally sons of this god. Humanity acquires a moral significance by the same stroke. Radicalising a universalist tendency already present in Stoicism,[15] the Christian doctrine proclaims the moral unity of mankind. 'It is indisputable', writes Olivier Mongin, 'that the egalitarianism which underlies the natural law of belonging to a human community cannot be separated from its Judaeo-Christian context, indeed from Evangelical values'.[16]

Although Christian love (*agapè*)[17] may well put the accent on the 'love of one's neighbour', by definition it never stops at the neighbour. Even if it can admit a hierarchy of pleasures or legitimate certain preferences, on the metaphysical level it does not know any borders. The neighbour, especially, is not so much 'loved' for himself as he is as a creature of God. In other words, he is loved only for that by which he does not differentiate himself fundamentally from other men — for that even which makes him similar to the others (the fact of having been created by God). Pierre Manent has clearly shown that there are two ways for a man to feel related to other men. The first, quite naturally, involves directing benevolence towards the one who has the most need of it, for example, towards the one who suffers. The relationship between men then derives from compassion. The second way is quite different: 'The relationship is not addressed to the visible and suffering body, it is addressed to something invisible, to the soul, if you like, more precisely to the *dignity* of the person'.[18] This way is the Christian way. Christian universalism, being unlimited, contains the seeds of all the later developments of the idea of fundamental equality. *Agapè* already announces the modern ideal of practical universal

---

15 Stoicism was a school of philosophy first developed in ancient Greece which taught that excessive emotion leads to errors in judgment. In this case, however, de Benoist is referring to the fact that the Stoics taught that all individuals, including slaves, were inherently equal before God and should be treated as such.-Ed.

16 'Droits de l'homme, une généalogique complexe', in *Projet*, September-October 1988, p. 53.

17 Classical Greek: 'love'. In Christianity, the word took on connotations of pure, divine love.-Ed.

18 'L'empire de la morale', in *Commentaire*, Autumn 2001, p. 503.

benevolence: all human beings should be treated with an equal respect to which their equal dignity gives them a right.

The Church proclaims the universal fraternity of men in Christ and their equality before God, but does not draw from it, originally, any particular message about the social organisation of humanity. Under the influence of Aristotle, Thomas Aquinas continues to profess the idea of an ordered cosmos and to relate the exercise of the law to the common good.

Another decisive stage is about to be opened with the appearance of the notion of subjective law. Historically this is bound to the rapid development, in the Middle Ages, of the nominalist[19] doctrine which, as a reaction to the theory of 'universals', claims that there is no being outside the individual being, that is to say, that there exist in the universe only individual beings. (This thesis is affirmed by William of Ockham[20] in the context of a famous theological debate bearing on the question of knowing how one can justify the property rights of the Franciscans when they have taken a vow of poverty.) Considering only the individual as existing, there results from this the fact that the collectivity is only a juxtaposition of individuals, the rights becoming naturally legitimate individual powers.

Nominalism maintains besides that the natural law is not so much the reflection of the divine *order* as of the divine *will*. Its partisans argue that a natural order which would indicate good and evil by itself would finally prevent God from deciding on good in a sovereign way. Taking into consideration the absolute freedom of God, it follows that no necessity is imposed by itself in nature, which permits William of Ockham to declare that the law is not a just relation between things but the reflection of a law willed by God. Thereby the universe is already emptied of sense and of its intrinsic *raison d'être*.

---

19 Nominalism denies that there is any such thing as a universal concept, maintaining that they are abstractions with no genuine reality.-Ed.

20 William of Ockham (c. 1288-c. 1348) was an English Franciscan friar who was asked to review the concept of Apostolic poverty in 1327, when some Franciscans asserted that since Jesus and his apostles had owned no personal property, and that therefore, in contrast to the wealth exhibited at the Vatican, friars should live by begging alone and that the fact that friars sometimes used property did not imply that they held ownership of property. He also maintained that the Pope himself was a heretic. This doctrine was not accepted by the Church. His text on this debate is 'A Letter to the Friars Manor'.-Ed.

Then there appears the Spanish Scholastic who, notably under the influence of political Augustiniansm, derived justice and law once again from norms derived from the moral law. (One will note that the term *justitia* is only derived relatively late from the Latin word *jus*: it is only from the Fourth century that the 'law' was related to 'justice' in the sense of a universal philosophical notion.) In the Sixteenth century, under the influence of the two principal representatives of the School of Salamanca,[21] Francisco de Vitoria and Francisco Suárez, Scholastic theology passes from a notion of objective natural law founded on the nature of things to a notion of a subjective natural law founded on individual reason. At the same time that he affirms the political unity of mankind, the Jesuit Francisco Suárez declares that social and political reality cannot be explained merely by the natural inclination to sociability: an act of will is also required of men, and is an accord of their wills. (The same idea was later taken up by Pufendorf.) Francisco de Vitoria adds that 'the right of people is what natural reason has established among all peoples'. Rights, then, become synonymous with an individual faculty conferred by the moral law, with a moral power of action. With subjective law, notes Michel Villey, the individual becomes 'the centre, the origin, of the legal universe'.[22]

This evolution, sketched rather rapidly, allows us to apprehend the fundamental difference existing between Classical natural law and modern natural law. While the nature of which the first natural law spoke was that of the cosmos which, as an extrinsic principle, defined an objective perspective, even though the law which was deduced from it was also an objective law, modern natural law is a subjective law wholly deducible from the subject. The principles which it enunciates, deduced from the rational nature of man, are the principles according to which men should live, independently of the existence of a particular society.

From a cosmological naturalism, one is thus, at first, passed to a theological naturalism. Then, in a later period, the justification of rights was no longer sought in the fact that all men have been 'created

---

21 The School of Salamanca refers to a theological school which flourished in Sixteenth-century Spain. The School addressed many issues, among them being the affirmation of the idea that private ownership of property is a right and that individuals have the right to enjoy that property independently of the needs of their community.-Ed.

22 *La formation de la pensée juridique modern* (Paris: Montchrétien, 1975), p. 663.

in the image of God' but in the nature of their nature. Right was no longer thought of as derived from the divine law but from human nature alone, characterised by reason. It was a revolution at the same time philosophical and methodological that will have immediate political consequences.

The first modern theoreticians of human rights argue in turn from the idea of a 'state of nature', an idea which one found already in the Sixteenth century in the Spanish Jesuit Mariana.[23] 'The right of nature, which writers commonly call *jus naturale*', writes Hobbes[24] at the opening of Chapter 14 of his *Leviathan*, 'is the liberty each man hath to use his own power as he will himself for the preservation of his own nature'.[25] 'Neither by the word *right* is anything signified', he adds elsewhere, 'than that liberty which every man hath to make use of his natural faculties according to right reason'.[26] In the state of nature, law is a power which man can make use of freely. And self-interest is the rule of this law. For Hobbes, as for Locke who permanently seeks his own self-interest, his advantage, his utility. It is therefore because he thinks he finds an advantage in it that he enters into contractual relations with others (to guarantee his right to property, according to Locke; in order to defend oneself against the hostility omnipresent in the state of nature, according to Hobbes).

Inheritor of nominalism, Hobbes also writes, 'But whatsoever is the object of many man's Appetite or Desire; that is it, which he for his part calleth *Good*'.[27] The formula is immediately reversed: the desire and the will of each individual determines his degree of good, and each individual is the sovereign judge of his own happiness.

---

23 Juan de Mariana (1536-1624), in *The King and the Education of the King*, asserts that following the Fall of Man, humanity in the 'state of nature' of absolute individual freedom, became increasingly subject to corruption, greed and violence which culminated in the wealthy and powerful realising that they could terrorise and exploit the weak through the construction of social hierarchies. The origins of society are therefore rooted in corruption rather than in an effort to improve the human situation.-Ed.

24 Thomas Hobbes (1588-1679) was an English political philosopher who laid many of the foundations of modern liberal societies.-Ed.

25 *Leviathan* (Cambridge: Cambridge University Press, 1991), p. 91.

26 *De cive, or The Citizen* (New York: Appleton-Century-Crofts, 1949), p. 27.

27 *Leviathan*, p. 39.

'In one way,' clarifies Charles Taylor, 'to speak of a universal, natural right to life does not seem much of an innovation… The earlier way of putting it was that there was a natural law against taking innocent life. Both formulations seem to prohibit the same things. But the difference lies not in what is forbidden but in the place of the subject. Law is what I must obey. It may confer on me certain benefits, here the immunity that my life, too, is to be respected; but fundamentally I am *under* law. By contrast, a subjective right is something which the possessor can and ought to act on to put it into effect.'[28]

The first rights are therefore, above all, rights to freedom. Equality is only the condition required for their realisation. This priority of freedom is simply explained. Freedom, the expression of a pure being in itself, an incarnation of the uniqueness of the individual, qualifies the nature of man independently of all social relations. Equality is certainly a correlation of freedom defined in this way (if everyone is comprised of a free and absolute desire to be oneself, then all are in a way identical) but, contrarily to freedom, it requires a minimum of social life to acquire a significance. In certain respects, as André Clair writes, it fulfils 'the function of an element that determines and transforms freedom; by this determination is formed the social relationship'.[29]

The existence of men being considered as having preceded their coexistence, the transformation of the simple plurality of individuals into a society should be explained. The traditional response is the contract or the market. Unlike an association in the biblical sense, the social contract is a pact contracted between equal partners. Following the example of business, it results from a calculation of self-interest. For Locke, the aim of all political association is economic: 'The great and chief end, therefore, of men's uniting into commonwealths, and putting themselves under government, is the preservation of their property'.[30] Possessed naturally, the rights are, besides, conceived on the model of the right to property. One understands that in the Seventeenth and Eighteenth centuries, the theory of rights was the privileged

---

28 *Sources of the Self: The Making of Modern Identity* (Cambridge: Cambridge University Press, 1989), p. 11.

29 *Droit, communauté et humanité* (Paris: Cerf, 2000), p. 62.

30 From *The Second Treatise of Government*, in *John Locke: Political Writings* (Indianapolis: Hackett Publishing, 2003), p. 73.

instrument used by the bourgeoisie to succeed in playing a political role proportionate to its economic weight.

But by the same token, politics loses its status of a cause to become an effect. The fact of society being no more than the consequence of a contract undertaken between individuals, power is no longer an organising force but a secondary product of society, a superstructure that is always threatening to the members of the society. (This role of superstructure, present among all liberal authors, will recur in Marx.) Concomitantly the political relationship is found to be entirely redefined on the basis of a new legal norm, corresponding to the subjective rights of the individual. Civil society, finally, is identified with the private sphere, that is to say, to that part of the society shielded from the political life, where individuals are thought to be able to act freely. 'The philosophical stake of modern natural law', writes Marcel Gauchet, '...is going to be the double redefinition of politics according to the subject: as regards the political element, the citizen, as the subject of individual right, and also, as regards the political whole, the political community, as the collective political subject'.[31]

Thus a triple revolution is accomplished. On the one hand, the notion of will is substituted for the notion of order. On the other hand, the individual has moved to the centre and the law has become his attribute. Finally, the law is identified with 'justice', the latter having henceforth an essentially moral complexion. With Hobbes and his successors, life in society is conceived in view of the utility of each at the heart of a world where nature as a unified totality has no more intrinsic value, nor significance, nor finality. Right is henceforth an individual property, a quality inherent in the subject, a moral faculty which grants permissions and authorises demands. Reason is conceived, fundamentally, as a simple faculty of calculation. The legal matter ceases to be the just solution (*dikaion*,[32] *id quod bonum est*),[33] and becomes an ensemble of sanctioned norms and conducts. The state and the law itself are no longer anything but instruments destined to guarantee individual rights and to serve the intentions of the contracting parties.

---

31 'Les tâches de la philosophie politique', in *La Revue du MAUSS*, first quarter 2002, p. 282.

32 Classical Greek: the exact meaning is disputed, but it generally means 'what is right'.-Ed.

33 Latin: 'that which is best'.-Ed.

'It is only by a strong usurpation at the same time furtive and violent', writes André Clair, 'that, at the turning point of the modern age, this mutation of the concept of right which has permitted the application of this concept to man has been accomplished; one then understood right as a property essentially present in every human being; instead of being a system of distributing and awarding lots among the members of a society (to the extent that it was defined primarily in terms of distributive justice), right is now conceived with a complete reversal of meaning as a faculty of affirming oneself that should be rendered absolutely effective for every individual *vis-à-vis* everybody else. Every philosophy of human rights is thus a philosophy of subjectivity, of a subjectivity of course said to be universal, but recognised initially as individual and unique.'[34]

If human rights are part of the law, the latter then has nothing more to do with what one understood by 'law' when the latter was founded. The classical natural law has been replaced by a modern natural law which argues from radically different theoretical bases, and does not have before it anything more than the platitude and manifest inadequacies of legal positivism.

In reality, as their theological roots demonstrate, human rights are only law contaminated by morality. But a morality which does not have anything to do with that of the Ancients, insofar as it no longer defines what it is *good to be*, but what it is *right to do*. Since the right precedes and commands the good, morality is no longer interested in what has a value in itself, or in what we should admire and love. It is henceforth interested only in that which is justifiable from the point of view of reason.

Such a morality derives from the biblical notion of 'justice'. It proposes a certain conception of 'justice' which, belonging by definition to the reign of ends, cannot constitute the specific aim of a politically determined activity. Bertrand de Jouvenel had already confirmed, with regard to the expression 'modern natural law', 'The key word which does not figure in the announcement is the word morality, and it is to this elided noun that the adjective 'natural' is related. When one speaks of natural law, one primarily understands that the foundation of positive law is in morality.'[35] Human rights constitute the legal custom of

---

34 *Droit, communauté et humanité*, pp. 63-64.

35 'L'idée du droit naturel', in *Le droit naturel* (Paris: PUF, 1959), p. 162.

a moral demand of 'justice'; they express a legal means of conceiving and expressing this morality. It is in this sense that, as Arnold Gehlen[36] was able to say, the diffusion of the discussion of human rights derives from the 'tyranny of moral hypertrophy.'[37]

The dream of a united humanity, subject to the same norms and living under the same Law, forms the basic fabric of this discussion. The ideology of human rights posits unified humanity at once as a given fact and as an ideal, as something that is and something that should be; in other words, as a sort of potential truth that cannot be verified and would appear fully only when it is realised. In such a perspective, the only differences admitted are 'differences within the same' (Marcel Gauchet). The other differences are denied or rejected for the sole reason that they cause one to doubt the same. The key word is that men are everywhere endowed with the same rights because, fundamentally, they are everywhere *the same*. In the final analysis, the ideology of human rights aims at subjecting all of humanity to a particular moral law rehabilitating the ideology of the Same.

*

Excursus: The Church and Human Rights

The theological roots of the ideology of human rights have been described many times. For a long time, however, as Jacques Maritain[38] wrote, 'the affirmation of rights themselves based on Christian principles appeared revolutionary with regard to the Christian tradition.'[39]

---

36 Arnold Gehlen (1904-1976) was a German philosopher who was active in the Conservative Revolution. He joined the Nazi Party in 1933 and remained in its ranks until the end of the war, being drafted into the Wehrmacht in 1943. After post-war denazification, he continued to write and teach, and his ideas remain influential on the German Right to this day.-Ed.

37 *Moral und Hypermoral: Eine pluralistische Ethik* (Frankfurt am Main: Athenäum, 1969), chapters 10 and 11. An analogous argument, founded on the critique of moral universalism, has been repeated more recently by Hans Magnus Enzensberger in *Civil Wars: From L.A. to Bosnia* (New York: The New Press, 1994).

38 Jacques Maritain (1882-1973) was a French Catholic philosopher who believed that Christian ethics are a necessary component of political systems.-Ed.

39 *Natural Law: Reflections on Theory and Practice* (South Bend: St. Augustine's Press, 2001), p. 79.

The reason for that is well-known. It rests, from the historical point of view, in the aggressive rationalist character of the modern formulation of these rights, in the climate of anti-clericalism that has surrounded their proclamation, as well as in the anti-religious persecutions of the Revolution[40] that followed it. Besides, from the doctrinal point of view, the Catholic critique could not admit the elimination of all dimensions of transcendence implied by the integral subjectivisation of rights, an elimination which tends to transfer to man a certain number of divine prerogatives, nor the fact that this subjectivisation opens the way to an unending demand which, not being founded on any standard, leads to relativism.[41]

On 23 April 1791, Pope Pius VI expressly condemned the Declaration of Rights of 1789, accusing the articles which composed it of being 'contrary to religion and society'. This condemnation was renewed for exactly a century. In 1832, for example, Gregory XVI qualified the theory of human rights as a 'veritable delirium', the same opinion being formulated again in the encyclical *Quanta Cura* of 1864.

Matters begin to evolve from the encyclical *Rerum Novarum* (1891) of Leo XIII. From this date, under the influence, most notably, of the thought of Father Luigi Taparelli d'Azeglio,[42] whose *Essai théorique sur le droit naturel* (1855) sought to give (or to give again) a theological content to subjective right, the notion of human rights begins to be introduced into the social thought of the Church.

Immediately after the Second World War, this development was rapidly accelerated. In 1963, in the encyclical *Pacem in Terris*, Pope John XXIII declared that he saw in the Universal Declaration of Human Rights of 1948 'a step in the right direction, an approach toward the establishment of a juridical and political ordering of the world community'

---

40 The French Revolution of 1789.-Ed.

41 Cf. Louis de Vaucelles, 'Les droits de l'homme, pierre d'achoppement', in *Projet*, September-October 1988, pp. 115-128.

42 Luigi Taparelli (1793-1862) was an Italian Jesuit scholar who was concerned with the Church's way of dealing with the social changes being brought about as a result of the Industrial Revolution. He is credited with coining the term 'social justice'. He viewed modern societies as being comprised of various sub-societies, with individuals belonging primarily to one of these rather than to society as a whole.-Ed.

(§ 144).[43] On 7 December 1965, the pastoral constitution *Gaudium et Spes*, adopted in the context of the Second Vatican Council, affirmed that 'the Church, therefore, by virtue of the Gospel committed to her, proclaims the rights of man; she acknowledges and greatly esteems the dynamic movements of today by which these rights are everywhere fostered.[44] Three years later, Paul VI declared in his turn, 'To speak of human rights is to affirm a common property of humanity.[45] In 1974, before the General Assembly of the United Nations, he specified, 'The Holy See gives its full moral support to the ideal contained in the Universal Declaration as to the progressive deepening of the human rights that are expressed therein.[46] John Paul II, finally, would declare in 1979 that the Universal Declaration of Human Rights 'is a milestone on the long and difficult path of the human race.[47]

The traditionalist Catholic milieus have, of course, interpreted this change as a sign, among others, of the 'rallying' of the Church to 'modern ideas.[48] Even though this point of view contains some truth, the reality is a little more complex. In declaring that it admits human rights, the Church understands above all that it recognises (and causes to be recognised) that part in their genealogy that returns to it. It does not, however, subscribe to the aspects which remain in its eyes con-

---

43 From the Vatican Web site (www.vatican.va/holy_father/john_xxiii/encyclicals/ documents/hf_j-xxiii_enc_11041963_pacem_en.html).-Ed.

44 From the Vatican Web site (www.vatican.va/archive/hist_councils/ii_vatican_ council/documents/vat-ii_cons_19651207_gaudium-et-spes_en.html).-Ed.

45 From a message delivered on the occasion of the 20th anniversary of the Declaration of Human Rights on 22 April 1968.-Ed.

46 From a message to the President of the 28th General Assembly of the United Nations on the occasion of the 25th anniversary of the Universal Declaration of Human Rights on 10 December 1973.

47 Cf. René Coste, *L'Église et les droits de l'homme* (Paris: Desclée, 1982); M. Simoulin, 'L'Église et les droits de l'homme', in *Les droits de l'homme*, special issue of *Vu de haut* (Escurolles: Fideliter, 1988); and Giorgio Filibeck, *Les droits de l'homme dans l'enseignement de l'Église, de Jean XXIII à Jean-Paul II* (Vatican City: Libreria Editrice Vaticana, 1992).

48 Cf. notably Jean Madiran, *Les droits de l'homme — DHSD* (Maule: Éditions de Présent, 1988) and *L'envers des droits de l'homme* (Issy-les-Moulineaux: Renaissance catholique, 1993). (The quote from John Paul II is from his address to the 34th General Assembly of the United Nations on 2 October 1979, available at the Vatican Web site [http://www.vatican.va/holy_father/john_paul_ii/speeches/1979/october/ documents/hf_jp-ii_spe_19791002_general-assembly-onu_en.html].-Ed.)

testable in their present formulation. In other words, the approval in principle given henceforth by the Church to the doctrine of human rights refers, first of all, to the Christian version of these rights. As François Vallançaon writes, 'The Church is no more for human rights than against them. It is favourable to human rights when they are well and rightly interpreted. It is hostile to them when they are badly and wrongly interpreted'.[49]

---

49 'Les droits de l'homme: analyse et critique', in *La Nef*, February 1999, p. 26.

▌▌

IN SEARCH OF A FOUNDATION

When UNESCO[1] had decided, in 1947, to launch a new Universal Declaration of Human Rights — the one, indeed, that would be solemnly proclaimed on the 10 December 1948 by the General Assembly of the United Nations — its directors undertook to proceed to a vast preliminary inquiry. Notably, at the initiative of Eleanor Roosevelt, an international committee was constituted in order to collect the opinions of a certain number of 'moral authorities'. Around 150 intellectuals from all countries were asked in this way to determine the philosophical basis of the new Declaration of Rights. This approach ended in failure, and its promoters had to limit themselves to registering the irreconcilable divergences between the responses obtained. Since no accord emerged, the Commission on Human Rights of the UN decided not to publish the results of this inquiry.

In his response, Jacques Maritain showed that he had no illusions, declaring that as regards human rights 'a *practical* accord is possible, [but] a *theoretical* accord is impossible among intellectuals'. It is, however, evident that it is difficult to speak of human rights without a precise conception of man considered as being the bearer of these rights. No consensus has ever been established on this point. Not having reached an accord, one thus decided to give up justifying what one wished to affirm. The authors of the Universal Declaration formulated its text in a consensual vision not corresponding to reality. 'The Declaration', affirms François Flahaut, 'had to be accepted by all on the condition that nobody ask what justifies it. That came back to a question of an imposition of authority'.[2]

---

1   United Nations Educational, Scientific and Cultural Organization.-Ed.

2   *Le sentiment d'exister: Ce soi qui ne va pas de soi* (Paris: Descartes et Cie, 2002), p. 453. Certain contributions to the debate opened by UNESCO were published in

René Cassin[3] was accustomed to saying that human rights rest 'on an act of faith in a better tomorrow and the destiny of man.'[4] Such an 'act of faith' would thus be justified by its aims. 'These aims', writes Julien Freund, 'we pose as norms, thus we affirm them dogmatically as valid and worthy of being pursued; they do not have the incontrovertible character of a scientific proposition.'[5] It results from this that the conception of man on which the theory of rights rests derives not from knowledge but from opinion. From this sole fact, in the manner of a religion — every belief is valid only to the exact extent to which one believes in it — they can have only a wishful validity, that is to say they are imposed only insofar as one accepts to see them imposed, and that they have no other validity but that which one decides to accord them. 'Every coherent reflection on human rights', repeats Julien Freund, 'can only proceed from the following fundamental fact: they have not been established scientifically, but dogmatically.'[6] 'Human rights', adds François de Smet, 'cannot escape their categorisation as an ideology. On account of this they are exposed to criticism.'[7]

Even the definition of man of which the theory of rights speaks is less evident than it appears. The proof of this is that many 'human rights' have been extended only progressively to women and to diverse other categories of human populations.[8] One may recall, as a symbol, that the two Western countries that vigorously maintained the institution of slavery for the longest time, France and the United States, are also those that were the first to proclaim human rights. Many of

---

English in 1949 (*Comments and Interpretations*) with an Introduction by Jacques Maritain. The work was republished by UNESCO in 1973.

3 René Cassin (1887-1976) was a French jurist and judge who helped to draft the Universal Declaration of Human Rights for the UN. A veteran of the First World War, he afterwards became a pacifist and was active in the League of Nations, the Consultative Council of Jewish Organisations, the UN's Human Rights Commission, and the European Court of Human Rights.-Ed.

4 From *Statement on the Implementation of Human Rights* (New York: United Nations, 1948).-Ed.

5 *Politique et impolitique* (Paris: Sirey, 1987), p. 192.

6 *Ibid.*, p. 189.

7 *Les droits de l'homme: Origines et aléas d'une idéologie moderne* (Paris: Cerf, 2001), p. 7.

8 On the late extension of human rights to women cf. notably Xavier Martin, *L'homme des droits de l'homme et sa compagne* (Bouère: Dominique Martin Morin, 2001).

the authors of the American Declaration of Independence of 1776, which included a defence of human rights, were, besides, themselves slave-owners.

There is not any more doctrinal or philosophical consensus as regards the definition of rights. 'A sort of vagueness envelops the notion itself of fundamental rights', the jurist Jean Rivero recognises.[9] When one speaks of a 'human right', does one mean that this right possesses an intrinsic value, an absolute value or an instrumental value? That it is of such importance that its realisation should take precedence over all other considerations, or that it just counts among the things that are indispensable? That it gives a power or a privilege? That it permits an immunity or that it confers an immunity? There are as many responses as there are questions.

The critiques of the theory of rights have often underlined its vague, but also contradictory character. For example, Taine[10] wrote about the Declaration of 1789, 'most of the articles are abstract dogmas, meta-physical definitions, more or less literary axioms, that is to say, more or less false, now vague and now contradictory, open to various interpretations and to opposite constructions, these are good for platform display but bad in practice, mere stage effect, a sort of pompous standard, useless and heavy...'[11] Analogous words are found in all the authors of the Counter-Revolution.

That there has always been disagreement concerning the scope and the content of human rights cannot be contested. Article 2 of the Declaration of 1789, for example, makes the right of 'resistance to oppression' one of the natural and inalienable rights.[12] Kant, on the other hand, denies the existence of such a right and goes so far as to advocate the duty of obedience to dictatorships.[13] He justifies this

---

9   In Louis Favoreu (ed.), *Cours constitutionnelles européennes et droits fondamentaux* (Paris: Presses universitaires d'Aix-Marseille, 1982), p. 521.

10 Hippolyte Taine (1828-1893) was a French historian and literary critic who was one of the chief influences on the Naturalist school. He opposed the ideals of the French Revolution, instead stressing the importance of race and regionalism.

11 *The French Revolution*, vol. 1 (New York: Henry Holt, 1878), p. 211.

12 One, however, does not see clearly how such a right could result from the purely individual nature of man, given that there could not be any 'oppression' outside an established public society.

13 Cf. 'Sur le lieu commun: c'est peut-être vrai en théorie, mains en pratique cela ne vaut point', in Kant, *Œuvres philosophiques*, vol. 3 (Paris: Gallimard-Pléiade, 1986),

denial by affirming that right cannot ever be effected except by the law, which means that a juridical state is possible only by submission to the legislative will of the state. (Natural law is here changed abruptly into positive law.) The Declaration of 1789 stipulates also, in the manner of Locke, that the right to property is 'inviolable and sacred'. The Declaration of 1948 is careful not to take this formula into account. The majority of the defenders of the rights of peoples to self-determination dissociate people and state, which is indispensable if one wishes to defend the rights of minorities. But Hans Kelsen,[14] theoretician of the state under the rule of law, expressly refuses this distinction. The principle of the non-retroactivity of the laws, held in 1789 as an inalienable right, has been abandoned regarding 'crimes against humanity'. Freedom of expression, guaranteed unconditionally in the United States as one of the human rights, is not in France, the other 'country of human rights', on the pretext that certain opinions do not merit being considered as such. It is equally possible in the United States to sell one's blood, whereas French law renders null and void any commercial contract related to a product of the human body. One can multiply the examples.

Human rights can also be shown to be internally self-contradictory. In a general way, it is common that rights originating from positive freedom come into contradiction with those that originate from negative freedom: the right to work, for example, can have as an obstacle the right to property or the right of free initiative. French law has, since 1975, guaranteed the right to abortion, but the text of the laws on bioethics adopted on 23 June 1994 at the National Assembly prohibits experiments on embryos, alleging the need for 'respect of the human being from the commencement of life'. If one believes that the embryo is not yet a human being, one fails to see why it would be prohibited to experiment on it. If one believes that it is, one fails to see how abortion can be justified.

How does one untangle in these conditions the 'true' rights from the 'false'? How does one prevent 'human rights' from becoming an

---

p. 265. (An abridged version of this essay appears in *The Theory of International Relations* [London: Allen & Unwin, 1970], as 'On the Commonplace: This is Perhaps True in Theory but in Practice it is Not Valid at All'.-Ed.)

14 Hans Kelsen (1881-1973) was an Austrian-Jewish jurist and legal scholar who is considered one of the most important legal philosophers of the Twentieth century. He was also considered to be the primary nemesis of Carl Schmitt.-Ed.

all-purpose expression, a mere *flatus vocis*[15] having only the ever-changing meaning that one attributes to it in one circumstance or another? Jean Rivero observes for his part that the 'major paradox of the fate of human rights for two centuries is doubtless the contrast between the withering of their ideological roots and the development of their content and their audience to a universal level.'[16] This is another way of saying that the more the discussion of human rights extends, the more the uncertainty regarding their nature and bases grows.

Now, this question of bases is posed nowadays with a quite particular acuteness. It is, in fact, only recently, as Marcel Gauchet says, that the problem of human rights 'has ended up leaving the books to make itself effective history.'[17] From the Nineteenth century, the fashionableness of the theory of human rights had been reduced, in fact suspended, under the influence of historicist theories, then revolutionary doctrines. To think in terms of the movement of history, in terms of progress, necessarily led to the relativisation of the importance of law. At the same time, the advent of historical time brought in a certain discrediting of the abstract intemporality characterising a 'state of nature' from whence the rights proceeded. The fall of the totalitarian regimes, the fading of revolutionary hopes, the crisis of all the representations of the future, and notably the idea of progress, have very logically coincided with a return of the ideology of rights with renewed force.

Historically, from 1970, human rights have been opposed to the Soviet system. Since the collapse of the latter — by a remarkable coincidence, the year of the fall of the Berlin Wall was also that of the bicentenary of the Declaration of 1789 — they have been employed in diverse ways to disqualify regimes or practices of all sorts, in particular in the Third World, but also to serve as a model for new national and international policies. The European Union has itself given them a position

---

15 The term *flatus vocis* was coined by the Medieval French nominalist theologian Roscellinus to describe his contention that only individuals exist, while terms which claim a universal truth are merely *flatus vocis*, or an emission of sound without any specific meaning, like a grunt.-Ed.

16 *Les droits de l'homme: droits individuels ou droits collectifs? Actes du Colloque de Strasbourg des 13 et 14 mars 1979* (Paris: Librairie générale de droit et de jurisprudence, 1980), p. 21.

17 'Les tâches de la philosophie politique', in *La Revue du MAUSS*, first quarter 2002, p. 279.

of the highest rank,[18] while, for some years, in authors like Rawls, Habermas, Dworkin and many others, one witnesses a new attempt at a foundation of the political community on law. The question of the foundation of human rights is thus posed anew.[19]

In its canonical version, in Locke as in Hobbes, the theory of rights 'proceeds by a mythical rationalisation of the origin. It projects into the abstract past of the state of nature, a past beyond history, the search for a primordial norm in itself atemporal with respect to the composition of the political body'.[20] One can qualify this procedure as cognitive-descriptive. Rights, in this view, are that which men are considered to 'possess' by virtue of the mere fact that they are men. The individual draws his inalienable rights, just as so many constituent attributes of his being, from the 'state of nature'. This is the classical legitimisation by human nature.

---

18 The Treaty of Maastricht (1992) stipulates that the European Union 'shall respect fundamental rights, as guaranteed by the European Convention for the Protection of Human Rights and Fundamental Freedoms signed in Rome on 4 November 1950'. The Treaty of Amsterdam (1997) takes a further step in adding that '[t]he Union is *founded* on the principles of liberty, democracy, respect for human rights and fundamental freedoms' (emphasis added). The European Community (and not the Union, which does not have a juridical character) had besides envisaged adhering to the European Convention of Human Rights. But a judgment rendered by the Court of European Justice on 28 March 1996 concluded that 'in the present state of community rights, the Community does not have the competence to adhere to the Convention'. Such an adhesion would have had as a consequence the placing of community institutions under the judicial tutelage of the Convention — beginning with the Court of Justice of Luxembourg, which would have found itself once again in a state of dependence on the Court of Strasbourg. That is the reason why the European Union, adopting a substitute solution, decided to announce a list of 'fundamental rights' protected by the Community's judicial order. This Charter of Fundamental Rights of the European Union, adopted by the European Council in 2000, comprises 54 articles preceded by a preamble. Its content reveals a vast syncretism of sources. As for its concrete value, it remains, at the moment, rather vague. The question of knowing if the Charter can be invoked before the national judge has, notably, not been decided. (The Charter was brought into force with the Treaty of Lisbon, which took effect on 1 December 2009.-Ed.)

19 Cf. notably Institut international de philosophie (ed.), *Les fondements des droits de l'homme: Actes des entretiens de l'Aquila, 14-19 septembre 1964* (Florence: Nuova Italia, 1966); and Mauricio Beuchot, *Los derechos humanos y su fundamentación filosófica* (Mexico: Universidad Iberoamericana, 1997).

20 Marcel Gauchet, *art. cit.*, p. 288.

This legitimisation appears clearly in the great basic texts. The American Declaration of Independence declares that all men are 'created equal', and that they are endowed by their Creator with a certain number of inalienable rights. The Universal Declaration of 1948 proclaims right from its first article: 'All human beings *are born* free and equal in dignity and in rights. They are *endowed* with reason and conscience'. It is because they are *natural* and *innate* that the rights are inalienable and inalterable.

Many defenders of the ideology of these rights still hold today to this reasoning. Francis Fukuyama, for example, affirms that 'any serious discussion of human rights must ultimately be based on some understanding of human ends or purposes, which in turn must almost always be based on a concept of human nature'.[21] According to him, only 'the existence of a single human nature shared by all the peoples of the world can provide, at least in theory, a common ground on which we can base universal human rights'.[22] That is why he remains a partisan of the use of the language of rights (*rights talk*), this being 'more democratic, universal and easily grasped'. He adds that the discourse on rights is valid because all men have the same preferences, which shows that they are 'in the end fundamentally similar'.[23] One finds this reasoning, of the Lockean type, again among conservatives like Tibor R. Machan,[24] Eric Mack, Douglas Rasmussen or Douglas J. Den Uyl, in a perspective which is also inspired by the libertarian Objectivism of Ayn Rand.[25]

This approach comes up against very great difficulties, beginning with the fact that there is no consensus on 'human nature'. In the course of history, the notion of 'nature' itself has been the object of the most contradictory definitions. For the Ancients, human nature orders the individuals according to the common good. For the Moderns, it legitimises their right to pursue all sorts of ends, with the result

---

21 'Natural Rights and Human History', in *The National Interest*, Summer 2001, p. 19 (available at www.allbusiness.com/government/3583877-1.html).

22 *Ibid.*, p. 24.

23 *Ibid.*, p. 30.

24 *Individuals and Their Rights* (La Salle, Illinois: Open Court, 1990).

25 Ayn Rand (1905-1982) was a Russian-American novelist and philosopher who promoted an extreme form of individualist capitalism which she termed Objectivism.-Ed.

that they fundamentally have only this right in common. Besides, once one has demonstrated that there exists a human nature, one has not at all demonstrated that it follows that man has rights in the sense which the doctrine of human rights gives to this word.

Hegel had already confirmed that it is difficult to invoke 'nature' to conclude from it the equality of men among themselves: 'We must rather say that by *nature* men are only *unequal*.'[26] The life sciences have not belied this point of view. The study of the biological nature of man, which has not ceased to progress in recent decades, shows that 'nature' is not very egalitarian and above all that, far from the individual being the basis of collective existence, it is much rather the collectivity which constitutes the basis of the existence of the individual: for Darwin, as for Aristotle, man is, first of all, by nature a social animal. In an article which caused a great sensation, Robin Fox wrote that one could also draw from this study of the biological nature of man conclusions going directly against the ideology of human rights, for example a legitimisation of murder, of vengeance, of nepotism, of arranged marriage or of rape: 'There is nothing in the "laws of nature" that says the kin group (the pool of genes related by descent) should not seek to enhance the reproductive success of its members.'[27] Fox drew the conclusion from this that the 'human rights' of which the ideology of human rights speaks either go against what one effectively observes in nature, or concern things on which nature says strictly nothing. One finds again a similar conclusion in Paul Ehrlich.[28] Baudelaire,[29] more radical, affirmed: 'Nature can counsel nothing but crime.'[30]

Another difficulty bears on the scope of what one can draw from a discovered fact. The liberal Anglo-Saxon tradition has not ceased affirming, following David Hume, G. E. Moore, R. M. Hare and some others, that one cannot derive conscience from being: the error of

---

26 *Hegel's Philosophy of Mind* (Oxford: Oxford University Press, 2007), p. 237.

27 'Human Nature and Human Rights', in *The National Interest*, New York, Winter 2000-2001, p. 81. Cf. also Robin Fox, 'Human Rights and Foreign Policy', in *The National Interest*, New York, Summer 2002, p. 120.

28 *Human Natures: Genes, Cultures, and the Human Prospect* (Washington: Island Press, 2000).

29 Charles Baudelaire (1821-1867) is regarded as one of the greatest French poets of the Nineteenth century and was a forerunner of the Symbolists.-Ed.

30 *The Painter of Modern Life and Other Essays* (London: Phaidon Press, 1995), p. 32.-Ed.

'naturalism'[31] (*naturalistic fancy*) would seem to consist in believing that nature can provide a philosophical justification to morality or law. This affirmation is extremely questionable, for reasons which we shall not demonstrate here. But from a liberal point of view, it comes into contradiction with the idea that the foundation of human rights is to be sought in human nature. To suppose, even in effect, that man ever had, in the 'state of nature', the characteristics which the ideology of rights attributes to him, if one cannot derive a conscience from being, if one cannot pass from an indicative finding to an imperative prescription, one cannot see how the fact of 'rights' can justify the demand to preserve them. Such is precisely the argument which Jeremy Bentham[32] opposed to human rights: taking into consideration the division between law and fact, even if human nature is what the partisans of the rights say of it, one cannot derive any prescription from it. The same argumentation is found again, in another perspective, in Hans Kelsen, as in Karl Popper.[33] It has been repeated, more recently, by Ernest van den Haag.[34]

The idea of a 'state of nature' having preceded any form of social life finally seems to be increasingly less tenable today. Certain defenders of human rights recognised it openly. Jürgen Habermas, for example, does not hesitate to say that 'the conception of human rights should be liberated from the metaphysical weight that is constituted by the hypothesis of an individual as existing before all socialisation, and coming into the world, as it were, with innate rights.'[35] One then tends to make of the isolated individual a necessary rational hypothesis or a useful narrative fiction. Rousseau[36] already evoked this state

---

31 In naturalism, it is maintained that all phenomena can be explained in terms of the forces of nature, and that there is nothing exterior to them, hence all supernatural or religious explanations are rejected.-Ed.

32 Jeremy Bentham (1748-1842) was an English jurist, social reformer and Utilitarian philosopher.-Ed.

33 *The Open Society and Its Enemies*, 2 vols. (London: Routledge & Kegan Paul, 1945). Popper considers that taking an example from nature inevitably leads to holism.

34 'Against Natural Rights', in *Policy Review*, Winter 1983, pp. 143-175.

35 'Le débat interculturel sur les droits de l'homme', in *L'intégration républicaine* (Paris: Fayard, 1998), p. 252.

36 Jean-Jacques Rousseau (1712-1778) was a philosopher who taught, among other things, that ethics stem from man's natural instincts rather than being ingrained

of nature that 'perhaps never did exist', but 'of which, it is, nevertheless, necessary to have true ideas'.[37] The state of nature is a 'necessary fiction' allowing one to imagine what the condition of men would be like before they are subjected to any form of obedience, that is to say, before any social relations. One deduces from it that, in such a state, they would be 'free and equal'. This is evidently pure speculation. 'Of course', writes Raymond Aron,[38] 'the formulas like "men are born free and equal in rights" do not stand up to scrutiny: "to be born free", in the proper sense, signifies nothing'.[39]

The discourse on human rights that has reappeared today is therefore much more problematic than that which was enunciated in the epoch of the Enlightenment. 'If there is a return of rights', observes Marcel Gauchet, 'it is a right without Nature. We have the content of subjective right without the support that permitted its elaboration'.[40] If human nature is not what one believed to know of it in the Eighteenth century, on what can one found the doctrine of natural rights? If the future of society no longer corresponds any longer to an emergence from the 'state of nature', how does one explain it in a way compatible with the theory of rights, that is to say with a theory centred on the individual?

Certain authors, like James Watson,[41] think that it would be better to stop reasoning in terms of the 'rights' of man and to limit oneself to speaking of 'needs' or of 'human interests'. But this method, which comes back to replacing the moral approach with an approach of a Utilitarian or consequentialist type, collides with the fact that no consensus can be established on the value of 'interests' or on the hierarchy

by society. Rousseau did not see society as evil, however, believing that injustice only came about with the development of social inequality in modern societies. He was very influential upon the French Revolution.-Ed.

37 *On the Origin of Inequality* (Chicago: Regnery, 1949), p. 17.-Ed.

38 Raymond Aron (1905-1983) was a prominent French-Jewish political philosopher who served in the Free French forces during the Second World War. Having a strong aversion to totalitarian systems, he opposed Marxism and those who were influenced by it, including his friend Jean-Paul Sartre.-Ed.

39 'Pensée sociologique et droits de l'homme', in *Études sociologiques* (Paris: PUF, 1988), p. 229.

40 *Art. cit.*, p. 288.

41 James Watson (b. 1936) is an English author of novels for young children. The quest for human rights is a frequent theme in his books.-Ed.

of 'needs', taking into account the eminently subjective and intrinsically conflicting character of these notions. Besides, interests are
by definition always negotiable, while values and rights are not (the
right to freedom cannot be reduced to the interest that an individual
may have in being free). Finally, human rights cannot be founded on
Utilitarianism,[42] since it posits as a principle that it is always legitimate to sacrifice certain men if this sacrifice allows one to increase the
'amount of happiness' of a greater number of men.[43]

A more ambitious alternative is that of Kantian philosophy, which
advocates a morality founded on the independence of the will. 'The
true moral choice', affirms Kant, 'implies the freedom of the will, that is
to say a free will which is self-determined in freeing itself of all natural
causality'. Defining as just every action 'insofar as it can coexist with
the freedom of every other in accordance with a universal law', Kant
makes freedom the sole 'original right belonging to every man by virtue of his humanity'.[44] In this view, the pure essence of law resides in
human rights, but the latter are no founded on human nature, but on
dignity (Würde). To respect the dignity of man is to respect the respect
of natural law which he bears in himself. 'Humanity itself is a dignity',
writes Kant, 'for a human being cannot be used merely as a means
by any human being (either by others or even by himself) but must
always be used at the same time as an end. It is just in this that his dignity (personality) consists, by which he raises himself above all other
beings in the world that are not human beings and yet can be used, and
so over all things'.[45]

Compared to the preceding theoreticians of human rights, the
change of perspective is radical. 'Originally', recalls Pierre Manent,

---

42 Utilitarianism is a philosophical school which has its origins in Nineteenth century
    England. There are many schools of Utilitarianism, but in essence it teaches that
    the morality of an action is determined by how likely it is to produce the greatest
    good for the greatest number of individuals. John Stuart Mill and Jeremy Bentham
    were prominent early exponents.-Ed.

43 On the critique of human rights by Jeremy Bentham, the founder of Utilitarianism,
    cf. Jeremy Waldron (ed.), 'Nonsense Upon Stilts': Bentham, Burke and Marx on the
    Rights of Man (London: Methuen, 1987); and Hugo Adam Bedau, '"Anarchical
    Fallacies": Bentham's Attack on Human Rights', in Human Rights Quarterly,
    February 2000, pp. 261-279.

44 Groundwork for the Metaphysics of Morals (Orchard Park: Broadview Press, 2005),
    p. 156.

45 Ibid., p. 173.

'human rights are the *natural* rights of man, those which are inscribed in his elementary nature... Human dignity, in contrast, is constituted, according to Kant, in holding a radical or essential distance in relation to the needs and desires of one's nature.'[46] The moral theory of Kant is in fact a deontological theory, that is to say, that it does not depend on any substantial proposition concerning human nature or the human aims which would derive from this nature. Reason no longer receives a substantial definition within it but a purely procedural definition, which means that the rational character of an agent is demonstrated by his manner of reasoning, by his manner of arriving at a result, and not by the fact that the result of his reasoning is substantially exact, in the sense of a conformity to an external order. Emanating from will alone, the moral law expresses the status of the rational agent. This is an extension of the Cartesian theory of a 'clear and distinct' thought, itself derived from the Augustinian conception of interiority. For Kant, the decisive procedure of reason is universalisation.From that time, not only are laws no longer derived from human nature, but they are in a certain way opposed to it. To act morally is to act according to duty, not by natural inclination. The moral law is no longer imposed from outside, it is prescribed by reason itself. The natural order no longer determines our ends and our normative objectives, we are henceforth obliged to produce the moral law from ourselves. That is why Kant recommends that one conform no longer to nature but to construct an image of things by following the canons of rational thought. Freedom, in Kant, is not a tendency or an attribute of human nature, but the very essence of human will — an absolutised faculty, detached from all contingency, a faculty permitting one to detach oneself from all forms of determinism and whose only criterion is the relationship to the moral universe of abstract humanism. (An idea rather close to the Calvinist doctrine: human nature is sinful, and the moral attitude consists in freeing oneself from all desire or natural tendency. One finds this idea already in Plato.) The abstraction of human rights, affirmed at an eminent level, thus places nature out of the picture. At the limit, humanity is defined as the capacity to free oneself from nature, to emancipate oneself from all natural determination, since every given *a priori* determination contradicts the independence of the will.

---

46 'L'empire de la morale', in *Commentaire*, Autumn 2001, p. 506.

This theory, which one finds also in John Rawls[47] and numerous other liberal authors, exposes itself to a well-known reproach: the principles having been posited *a priori*, how can one be sure that they are applicable to empirical reality? And how does one reconcile the reconcile the disregard for human nature with the findings of the life sciences, which establish its reality with ever-increasing force?[48] Hegel had already underlined that Kantian universalism, in failing to take into account social morality (*Sittlichkeit*), that is to say, the collection of moral obligations towards the community to which one belongs which results from the sole fact of belonging to it — obligations largely founded on established customs and practices — is incapable of supplying concrete norms for action. Remaining powerless to fix contents to duty and to distinguish morally good actions, it does not succeed in departing from a formal subjectivism. Moral autonomy is thus acquired only at the expense of emptiness: the ideal of detachment refers back to a freedom sought for itself, to a freedom without content. But the same ideal refers back also to a certain ethnocentrism, for there cannot be formal and procedural rights which do not imply, in a surreptitious way, a substantial content: 'The declaration of right is also an affirmation of value' (Charles Taylor). Liberal ethics is characterised collectively by the search for a formal principle, axiologically neutral, which can constitute a universalisable criterion. This axiological neutrality is always artificial.

As for reason, it too can only remain mute about its own foundations. Alasdair MacIntyre has shown that it is never neutral or atemporal, but, on the contrary, always tied to a cultural and socio-historical

---

47 Related to this is the fact that, like many other adherents of a deontological morality (Ronald Dworkin, Bruce Ackerman, etc.), Rawls surreptitiously reintroduces into his discourse a certain number of considerations referring, in spite of everything, to human nature (particularly when, evoking the hypothetical 'veil of ignorance' which is said to characterise the 'original position', he lends man an innate tendency to refuse risk).

48 Under the influence of Kant or the empiricism of the *tabula rasa*, there are numerous authors who have, from these assumptions, quite simply denied the existence of a human nature. Cf., in the very first place, the very critical work of Steven Pinker, *The Blank State: The Modern Denial of Human Nature* (New York: Viking Press, 2002), which has already given rise in Anglo-Saxon countries to a debate of the widest scope. Pinker sees in human nature, which he wishes to rehabilitate, a veritable 'modern taboo'.

context.[49] Kantian reason believes that it is able to recognise a universal law, that is to say, a world that would be external to it, when it can never produce it except from itself. Always dependent on its particular incarnations, it cannot be disassociated from a plurality of traditions. The notion of dignity is not less equivocal. We know that the modern theoreticians of human rights, even when they do not refer explicitly to the philosophy of Kant, make great use of it.[50] The word 'dignity', absent from the Declaration of Rights of 1789, figures in the preamble of the Universal Declaration of 1948 which expressly evokes 'the dignity inherent in all the members of the human family'. This dignity is evidently the character of an abstract humanity. It 'is always attached to the intrinsic humanity freed of all socially imposed regulation or norm', writes Peter Berger.[51] We know that, historically, dignity, attributed to everybody, has replaced honour, which is only present in some.

In its present definition, the term possesses a certain religious resonance. The idea of a dignity that is equal in every man belongs in fact neither to legal language nor to political parlance, but to the language of morality. In the biblical tradition, dignity has a precise meaning: it elevates man above the rest of Creation, it assigns to him a separate status. It posits him, as the sole titular of a soul, as radically superior to other living beings.[52] It also has an egalitarian significance, since no man can be regarded as more or less worthy than another. That means that dignity has nothing to do with the merits or the qualities which are proper to each person, but that it already constitutes an attribute of human nature. This equality is placed in relation to the existence of a single god: all men are 'brothers' because they have the same Father (*Malachi* 2:10), and because they have all been created 'in the image of God' (*Genesis* 9:6). As the *Mishnah*[53] says, 'Man was created as a single

---

49 *Whose Justice? Which Rationality?* (Notre Dame: University of Notre Dame Press, 1988).

50 Cf., notably, Myres S. McDougal, Harold D. Lasswell and Lung-chu Chen, *Human Rights and World Public Order* (New Haven: Yale University Press, 1980).

51 'On the Obsolescence of the Concept of Honour', in Stanley Hauerwas and Alasdair MacIntyre (eds.), *Revisions* (Notre Dame: University of Notre Dame Press, 1983).

52 Cf. Alain Goldmann, 'Les sources bibliques des droits de l'homme', in Shmuel Trigano (ed.), *Y a-t-il une morale judéo-chrétienne?* (Paris: In Press, 2000), pp. 155-164.

53 The *Mishnah* is a collection of debates which were discussed by ancient rabbis, and comprises part of what is known as the *Oral Torah*, since it was initially passed

specimen so that nobody can say to the other: my father is superior to yours' (*Sanhedrin* 4:5). Although insisting on love more than on justice, Christianity has taken responsibility for the same idea: dignity is, first of all, the quality by which man can rightly be posited as the master of those without a soul, the centre of Creation.

In Descartes, the affirmation of human dignity is developed from the evaluation of interiority as a place of self-sufficiency, as a place of the autonomous power of reason. In the Moderns, dignity is always an attribute, but instead of this attribute being received from God, it becomes a characteristic trait that man possesses directly from his nature. Finally, in Kant, dignity is directly associated with moral respect. 'One could say', writes Pierre Manent, 'that the Kantian conception is a radicalisation, and therefore a transformation, of the Christian conception that St. Thomas Aquinas in particular had stressed. If, for St. Thomas Aquinas, human dignity consists in freely obeying the natural and divine law, for Kant it consists in obeying the law which man gives to himself'.[54]

Whatever the meaning one gives to it, dignity becomes problematic as soon as one posits it as an absolute. One understands what being 'worthy of' means relative to such and such a thing, but 'worthy' in itself? Is dignity, such as the theory of rights conceives it, a right or a fact? A quality of nature or of reason? In Rome, *dignitas* was closely bound to a relation of comparison necessary to determine the qualities that caused one to merit something, to be worthy. Cicero: *Dignitas est alicujus honesta et cultu et honore et verecundia digna auctoritas.*[55] In this view, evidently dignity could not be equally present in everybody.[56] Modern dignity, on the contrary, is an attribute which cannot be increased or decreased since it is the reality of everyone. The man who is worthy is no longer opposed to the man who is unworthy, and the 'dignity of man' becomes a pleonasm since it is the fact of being a man, whoever one may be, that makes one worthy. However, if man

---

down orally before being transcribed.-Ed.

54 *Art. cit.*, p. 505.

55 'Dignity is the honourable authority of a person, combined with attention and honour and worthy respect paid to him'. Cicero, 'De Inventione', in *The Orations of Marcus Tullius Cicero* (London : H. G. Bohn, 1856), vol. 4, Book 2, Chapter 55, p. 376.-Ed.

56 A distant echo of this hierarchy is found in Christian theology when it distinguishes the 'perfect dignity' of Christians from the 'imperfect dignity' of the non-baptised.

should be respected by virtue of his dignity and what his dignity is based on is his right to respect, one is in a circular argument.[57] Finally, if everybody is worthy, it is as if nobody were: the factors of distinction must simply be sought elsewhere.

Conscious of the difficulties that the legitimation of human rights by human nature raises, the modern heirs of Kant[58] abandon their cognitivistic type of method in order to adopt a prescriptivist approach. But then, strictly, the rights that they defend are no longer rights. They are only moral exigencies, 'human ideals' which represent, at best, only what one needs to posit as rights to arrive at a social state judged, rightly or wrongly, as desirable or better. They then lose all compelling force, for ideals do not in themselves confer any right.[59]

Another manner of founding human rights consists in making them rest on the fact of belonging to the human species. Humanity, as in the Bible, is then presented as a 'big family', all the members of which would be 'brothers'. Those who adopt this method observe that all men are related to one another, from the fact of their common membership in the human species. They then affirm that it is on the foundation of this relationship that one should attribute to them or recognise in them the same rights. André Clair thus proposes to make human rights rest not on equality or freedom but on the 'third right' of fraternity. By the same stroke, the individualist charge of the Classical theory of rights would find itself defused: 'If one thinks of fraternity in relation to paternity, one finds oneself engaged in a new problem which is no longer that of human rights in the habitual sense (subjective), but that of the rooting in a lineage or tradition.'[60]

This method is interesting but it is faced, in turn, with insurmountable difficulties. First of all, it squarely contradicts the doctrine according to which human rights are fundamentally individual rights, the source of these rights being the individual considered in himself, not

57 Cf. Jacques Maritain, *Les droits de l'homme* (Paris: Desclée de Brouwer, 1989), pp. 69-72.

58 We may cite, for example, A. I. Melden, *Rights and Persons* (Oxford: Oxford University Press, 1972); and Joel Feinberg, *Rights, Justice, and the Bounds of Liberty* (Princeton: Princeton University Press, 1980).

59 Cf. on this subject S. S. Rama Rao Pappu, 'Human Rights and Human Obligations: An East-West Perspective', in *Philosophy and Social Action*, November/December 1982, p. 20.

60 *Droit, communauté et humanité* (Paris: Cerf, 2000), p. 67.

according to his history, his associations or his genealogy. Now, from the mere belonging to the species, it is evidently easier to derive collective rights than individual rights. To this contradiction is added another, insofar as fraternity is defined above all not as a right, but as a duty that is only apprehended in a normative mode of the relationship to others: to say that all men are brothers only means that they *should* all consider themselves as such.

The ideological bible of human rights stipulates explicitly that the rights of which it speaks are those of man in himself, that is to say, of a man divested of all his associations. From this it is deduced that the moral status (rights) can never be the function of membership in a group. Now, humanity indeed constitutes a group. The question is then of knowing why one recognises in this group a moral value that one denies to infraspecific examples, and why one affirms that all associations should be held as invalid even while considering one, the membership in humanity, as decisive. Jenny Teichmann, who is one of the authors who seek to base such rights on membership in the human species, writes that 'it is natural for gregarious beings to prefer the members of their own species, and humans are not an exception to this rule'.[61] But would why this preference, legitimate at the level of the species, not be so at other levels? If the moral agents are allowed to concede a preferential treatment on the basis of the relative proximity created by a common association, or by the particular type of relations which result from it, why could this attitude not be generalised? One can certainly reply that the membership in the species takes precedence over the others because it is the largest, that it encompasses all the others. That does not explain why all the possible associations should be delegitimised in favour of that which outclasses them, nor why that which is true at one level should cease to be so at another.

The biological definition of man as a member of the human species is, besides, just as conventional or arbitrary as the others: it rests on the sole criterion of specific interfecundity. However, the evolution of the legislation on abortion has led one to understand that an embryo is a human being only potentially and not in act. The underlying idea is that the definition of man by biological factors alone does not suffice. One therefore tried to go beyond that, by emphasising that it is not only because they belong to another species that men are distinguished

---

61 *Social Ethics: A Student's Guide* (Oxford: Basil Blackwell, 1996), p. 44.

from the rest of living beings, but also and above all by an entire collection of capacities and characteristics that are typical of them. The inconvenience is that, whatever the capacity or characteristic retained, it is improbable that it is found equally present in everyone. To define, for example, membership in the human species by the self-consciousness or the capacity of positing oneself as a subject of rights, immediately poses the problem of the status of children at a young age, of senile old people and severely handicapped people.

It is precisely this double contradiction that those who fight for 'animal rights' have not failed to exploit, and even to the point of attempting to grant human rights to the great apes. Denouncing as 'speciesist' the doctrine according to which only humans should be recognised as possessors of rights, they consider that there is nothing moral in attributing a particular moral status to living beings on the basis of their membership in a group alone, in this case the human species. They affirm on the other hand that the great apes belong to the 'moral community' to the extent that they possess, at least in a rudimentary state, characteristics (self-consciousness, moral sense, elementary language, cognitive intelligence) that certain 'non-paradigmatic' humans (the severely handicapped, disabled, senile, etc.) do not possess or no longer possess. In other words, against the partisans of the Classical theory of human rights, they return the argument used by the latter to discredit infraspecific memberships.

'To attribute a special value or special rights to the members of the human species based on the sole fact that they are members of it', writes Elvio Baccarini, 'is a morally arbitrary position which cannot be distinguished from sexism, racism or ethnocentrism.'[62] 'Are we disposed', adds Paola Cavalieri, 'to say that the genetic relationship which the membership in a race implies justifies according a particular moral status to the other members of one's race? The negative response leads thus to a rejection of the defence of humanism based on relationship.'[63]

---

62 'On Speciesism', in *Synthesis Philosophica*, 2000, issue 1-2, p. 107.

63 'Les droits de l'home pour les grands singes non humains?', in *Le Débat*, January/February 2000, p. 159. Cf., in the same issue, the speeches of Luc Ferry, Marie-Angèle Hermitte and Joëlle Proust. Cf. also Peter Singer, *Animal Liberation* (New York: New York Review of Books, 1990); and Paola Cavalieri and Peter Singer, *The Great Ape Project: Equality Beyond Humanity* (New York: St. Martin's Press, 1994). An analogous argument had been maintained in the past, but in a humorous manner, by Clément Rosset in *Lettre sur les chimpanzés* (Paris: Gallimard, 1965).

The classical response to this sort of argument, which rest on the deconstruction of the notion of humanity by recourse to the idea of biological continuity among the living, is that the animals can be objects of right (we have duties with regard to them), but not subjects of right. Another reply consists in deepening the notion of the human species, a third in pushing the reasoning *ad absurdum*: why stop at the great apes and not attribute the same 'rights' to felines, to mammals, to insects, to paramecia? The discussion can in fact only come to a sudden end insofar as the problem is posed in terms of 'rights'.

Pope John Paul II, in the encyclical *Evangelium Vitae*, affirms for his part that all men and only men are proprietors of rights, for they are the only beings capable of recognising and adoring their Creator. This affirmation, apart from being based on a belief that one is not obliged to share, comes up against the objection already mentioned above: according to all evidence, neither the newborn nor the old afflicted with Alzheimer's disease, nor the mentally ill, are capable of 'recognising and adoring' God.Certain authors do not, for all that, consider it less necessary to recognise that the basis of the ideology of human rights is inevitably religious. Michael Perry, for example, writes that there is no positive reason to defend human rights if one does not posit straightaway that human life is 'sacred'.[64] This affirmation makes one think when it emanates, as it often does, from a declared atheist. Alain Renaut has, not without reason, mocked these theoreticians who, after having decreed the 'death of man', nonetheless defend human rights, that is to say the rights of a being whose disappearance they themselves have proclaimed. The spectacle of those who profess the 'sacred' character of human rights, even while flattering themselves for having suppressed all forms of the sacred in social life, is no less comical.

Quite at the other extreme, certain people think, on the contrary, that the defence of human rights does not need any metaphysical or moral foundation. For Michael Ignatieff, it is useless to search for a justification of rights in human nature, just as it is unnecessary to say that

---

Princess Stéphanie of Monaco did not hesitate to declare, 'Animals are men like the others'. A Universal Declaration of Animal Rights was proclaimed on 15 October 1978 at UNESCO. Its first article affirms that 'All animals have equal rights to exist within the context of biological equilibrium'.

64 *The Idea of Human Rights: Four Inquiries* (New York: Oxford University Press, 1998), pp. 11-41. Cf. also Liam Gearon (ed.), *Human Rights and Religion: A Reader* (Brighton: Sussex Academic Press, 2002).

these rights are 'sacred'.[65] It is enough to take into account what the individuals consider in general to be right. William F. Schulz, executive director of Amnesty International, also assures us that human rights are nothing else than what men declare to be rights.[66] A. J. M. Milne, in a similar manner, tries to define human rights based on a 'minimum standard' determined by certain moral exigencies proper to all social life.[67] Rick Johnstone writes that 'human rights do not "win" because they are "true" but because the majority of men have learned that they are better than others'.[68] These modest propositions, of a pragmatic character, are not very convincing. To consider that rights are nothing else but what men consider to be rights is tantamount to saying that the rights are of an essentially procedural nature. The risk is then great of causing the definition of human rights to fluctuate according to the subjective opinions of each person. That amounts, at the same time, to transforming natural rights into vague ideas or into positive rights. Now, positive rights are still less 'universal' than natural rights, since it is often in the name of a particular positive right that the discussion of human rights is challenged.

Guido Calogero indeed considers that the idea of a *foundation* of human rights should be abandoned in favour of one of an argumentative justification of it.[69] But he admits that this proposition is hardly satisfying, for it causes the 'truth' of human rights to depend on the argumentative capacity of interlocutors alone, this being always suspended by new possible arguments. The search for the justification of human rights then returns to the argumentative search for a new intersubjective, and therefore necessarily provisional, consensus, in a perspective which does not fail to recall the communicative ethics of Jürgen Habermas.[70] Norberto Bobbio, finally, maintains that a philosophical or

65 *Human Rights as Politics and Idolatry* (Princeton: Princeton University Press, 2001).

66 *In Our Own Best Interest: How Defending Human Rights Benefit Us All* (New York: Beacon Press, 2002).

67 *Human Rights and Human Diversity: An Essay in the Philosophy of Human Rights* (London: Macmillan, 1986).

68 'Liberalism, Absolutism, and Human Rights: Reply to Paul Gottfried', in *Telos* 116, Summer 1999, p. 140.

69 'Il fondamento dei diritti dell'uomo', in *La Cultura*, 1964, p. 570.

70 For Habermas, the agent is above all constituted by language, thus by communicative exchange. Reason is made to progress via the means of a consensus obtained

argumentative foundation of human rights is quite simply impossible, and besides useless.[71] He justifies this opinion by affirming that human rights, far from forming a coherent and precise whole, have historically had a variable content. He admits that a number of these rights can be mutually contradictory and that the theory of human rights comes up against all the aporias of foundationalism,[72] for no consensus will ever be able to establish itself on the initial postulates. A rather similar point of view has been expressed by Chaïm Perelman.[73]

Whether one alleges human nature or reason, the dignity of man or his belonging to humanity, the difficulty of establishing the foundations of human rights thus reveals itself to be insurmountable. But if human rights are not based upon truth, their scope is found to be strongly limited as a consequence. They are no more than 'consequences without premises', as Spinoza[74] would have said. In the final analysis, the theory comes back to saying that it is preferable not to suffer oppression, that freedom is better than tyranny, that it is not good to do bad to people, and that persons should be considered as persons rather than as objects, all things that one could not contest. Was such a detour necessary to arrive at this point?

---

through discussion. Cf. *The Theory of Communicative Action*, 2 vols. (Boston: Beacon Press, 1984, 1987). Habermas proposes to redefine human rights starting with respect for the subject as the basis of 'communicative activity'. He denies on the other hand that human rights are of a moral nature, adding, however, that 'what confers on them the appearance of moral rights is not their content...but the sense of their validity, which surpasses the judicial system of the United Nations' (*La paix perpétuelle: Le bicentenaire d'une idée kantienne* [Paris: Cerf, 1996], p. 86).

71 *Per una teoria generale della politica* (Turin: Einaudi, 1999), pp. 421-466.

72 Foundationalism is an epistemological theory which holds that all beliefs are founded on the suppositions of what are termed 'basic beliefs'. Basic beliefs are said to be derived directly through experience and thus are self-evident, not relying on other beliefs for support.-Ed.

73 Chaïm Perelman (1912-1984) was a Polish-Jewish legal philosopher who lived most of his life in Belgium. In his work he attempted to navigate a middle road between scepticism and positivism. He is also regarded as one of the most important theoreticians of rhetoric in the Twentieth century.-Ed.

74 Baruch Spinoza (1632-1677) was a Dutch Jewish philosopher who is regarded as one of the greatest philosophers of all time. He makes this remark in relation to 'confused ideas' in his *Ethics*, Part Two, Proposition 28.-Ed.

III

HUMAN RIGHTS
AND CULTURAL DIVERSITY

*Human rights are only universal if they include the right not to believe
in the dogma of the universality of rights. — Giuliano Ferrara*[1]

The theory of human rights is given as a theory valid for all time and
for all places, that is to say, as a universal theory. This universality,
reputedly inherent in each individual posited as a subject, represents
in it the standard applicable to all empirical reality. In such a view, to
say that the rights are 'universal' is only another way of saying that they
are absolutely true. At the same time, everybody knows well that the
ideology of human rights is a product of the thought of the Enlightenment, and that the very idea of human rights belongs to the specific
context of Western modernity. The question then arises of knowing if
the narrowly circumscribed origin of this ideology does not implicitly contradict its pretensions to universality. Since every declaration
of rights is historically dated, does not a tension, or a contradiction
result from it, between the historical contingency that presided at its
elaboration and the demand of universality which it intends to affirm?

It is clear that the theory of rights, with respect to all human cultures, represents the exception rather than the rule — and that it even
constitutes exception within European culture, since it appeared only
at a definite moment and relatively late in the history of this culture.
If the rights have been 'there' always, present in the very nature itself
of man, one may be surprised that only a small portion of humanity
has perceived it, and that it has taken it so long to be perceived. How
does one understand that the universal character of rights appeared

---

1   *Il Foglio*, 23 December 2002.

as something 'evident' only in a particular society? And how does one imagine that this society could proclaim its universal character without at the same time vindicating its historical monopoly? That is to say, without positing itself as superior to those who have not recognised it?

The notion of universality itself raises problems. When one speaks of the universality of rights, of what type of universality does one wish to speak? Of a universality of a geographical, philosophical or moral order? The universality of rights, besides, comes up against this question, posed straightaway by Raimundo Panikkar: 'Is there any sense in asking oneself if the conditions of universality are unified when the question of universality itself is far from being a universal question?'[2]

To say that all men are possessors of the same rights is one thing. To say that these rights should be recognised everywhere under the form that the ideology of rights gives it is another, quite different thing. That raises, in fact, the question of knowing who has the authority of imposing this point of view, what is the nature of this authority, and what guarantees the soundness of his discourse. In other words: who decides that it should be thus and not otherwise?

All universalism tends towards the neglect or effacement of differences. In its canonical formulation, the theory of rights itself seems little disposed to recognise cultural diversity, and this is the case for two reasons: on the one hand its fundamental individualism, and the highly abstract character of the subject whose rights it proclaims, and on the other hand its privileged historical links with Western culture, or at least with one of the constituent traditions of this culture. One had a perfect illustration of that when the French Revolution affirmed the necessity of 'refusing everything to the Jews as a nation and according everything to them as individuals', which came to link the emancipation of the Jews to the disintegration of their communal links.[3] Since

---

2   'La notion des droits de l'homme est-elle un concept occidental?', in *Diogène*, Paris, October-December 1982, p. 88. This text was republished in *La Revue du MAUSS*, Paris, first quarter 1999, pp. 211-235.

3   Shortly following the French Revolution in 1789, the National Assembly declared Jews to hold the same rights as French citizens, making France the first European nation to do so. However, the Jews were no longer recognised as a distinct community, but rather as just one of several religions in France who should be subject to the same laws and authorities as all other citizens. The quotation is from Stanislas Marie Adélaïde, comte de Clermont-Tonnerre (1757-1792), a French nobleman who became the spokesman for those nobles who joined the Third Estate following the Revolution. He made this statement in his 'Speech on

then, the discourse of human rights has not ceased to be confronted by human diversity such as is expressed in the plurality of political systems, of religious systems and of cultural values. Is this discourse dedicated to dissolving them or can it subsume them at the risk of dissolving itself? Is it compatible with the differences or can it only try to make them disappear?

All these questions, which have given rise to a considerable amount of literature,[4] end, in the final analysis, in a simple alternative: that is, one maintains that the constituent concepts of the ideology of human rights are, in spite of their Western origin, truly universal concepts. Then one has to demonstrate this. Or one should give up their universality, which would ruin the entire system: in fact, if the notion of human rights is purely Western, then its universalisation at the planetary level patently represents an imposition from outside, a devious way of converting and dominating, that is to say a continuation of the colonial syndrome.

An initial difficulty appears already at the level of vocabulary. Up until the Middle Ages, one does not find in any European language — not more than in Arabic, Hebrew, Chinese or Japanese — a term designating *a* right as the subjective attribute of the person, distinct in itself from the judicial matter (*the* law). Which is the same as

---

Religious Minorities and Questionable Professions', which he delivered in the National Assembly on 23 December 1789.-Ed.

4   On the difficult question of knowing how one can reconcile individual rights with collective rights on the one hand with the rights of the peoples to self-determination and the respect of the cultural diversity of others on the other, cf. notably *Les droits culturels en tant que droits de l'homme* (Paris: UNESCO, 1970); A. J. M. Milne, *Human Rights and Human Diversity: An Essay in the Philosophy of Human Rights* (London: Macmillan, 1986); Ludger Kühnhardt, *Die Universalität der Menschenrechte: Studie zur ideengeschichtlichen Bestimmung eines politisches Schlüsselbegriffs* (Munich: Günter Olzog, 1987); Alison Dundes Renteln, *International Human Rights: Universalism versus Relativism* (London-Newbury Park: Sage, 1990); Wolfgang Schmale (ed.), *Human Rights and Cultural Diversity* (Goldbach: Keip, 1993); and Eva Brems, *Human Rights: Universality and Diversity* (The Hague: Martinus Nijhoff, 2001). Cf. also Adamantia Pollis and Peter Schwab, 'Human Rights: A Western Construct with Limited Applicability?', in A. Pollis and P. Schwab (eds.), *Human Rights: Cultural and Ideological Perspectives* (New York: Praeger, 1980), pp. 1-18; and Axel Honneth, 'Is Universalism a Moral Trap? The Presuppositions and Limits of a Politics of Human Rights', in James Bohman and Matthias Lutz-Bachmann (eds.), *Perpetual Peace: Essays on Kant's Cosmopolitan Ideal* (Cambridge, Massachusetts: MIT Press, 1997), pp. 155-178.

saying that, until a relatively late period, there did not exist any word to designate these rights considered as belonging to men by virtue of their humanity alone. This fact alone, judges Alasdair MacIntyre, leads one to doubt their reality.[5]

The very notion of right is not in the least universal. The Indian language has to only approximate equivalents to express it, such as *yukta* and *ucita* (appropriate), *nyayata* (just) or again *dharma* (obligation). In Chinese, 'right' is translated by the juxtaposition of two words, *chuan li*, indicating power and interest. In Arabic, the word *haqq*, 'right', means, first of all, truth.[6]

The theory of human rights postulates, besides, the existence of another universal human nature, independent of epochs and places, which would be recognisable by means of reason. Of this affirmation, which does not belong to it properly (and which in itself is in no way contestable), it gives a very particular interpretation implying a triple separation: between man and other living beings (man is the sole possessor of natural rights), between man and society (the human being is fundamentally the individual, and the social fact is not pertinent for knowing his nature), and between man and the cosmic whole (human nature does not owe anything to the general order of things). Now, this triple separation does not exist in the vast majority of non-Western cultures, including of course those which recognise the existence of a human nature.

The problem comes up quite particularly in the case of individualism. In the majority of cultures — as besides, one must recall, in the original Western culture — the individual in himself is quite simply not representable. He is never conceived as a monad, cut off from what connects him not only to his immediate neighbours, but to the community of living beings and to the entire universe. The notions of order, justice and harmony are not elaborated from him, nor from the individual place which would be that of man in the world, but from the group, the tradition, and the social relations, or the totality of reality. To speak of the freedom of the individual in himself thus makes no sense in the cultures which have remained fundamentally holistic, and which refuse to conceive of the human being as a self-sufficient atom.

---

5   *After Virtue: A Study in Moral Theory* (Notre Dame: University of Notre Dame Press, 1981), pp. 69-70.

6   Cf. Georges H. Bousquet, *Précis de droit musulman* (Paris: Armand Colin, 1963).

In these cultures, the notion of subjective rights is absent, whereas those of mutual obligation and reciprocity are omnipresent. The individual does not have to justify his rights but to work to find in the world, and first of all in the society to which he belongs, the most propitious conditions for the realisation of his nature and the excellence of his being.

Asiatic thought, for example, is expressed above all in the language of duties. The basic moral notion of Chinese thought is that of the duties which one has towards others, not that of the rights that one could oppose to them, for 'the world of duties is logically anterior to the world of rights'.[7] In the Confucian tradition, which cultivates the harmony between beings and nature, the individual could not possess rights superior to the community to which he belongs. Men are related to each other by the reciprocity of duties and mutual obligation. The world of duties is, besides, more extended than that of rights. While there is a theoretical correspondence between each right and a duty, it is not true that to each obligation there corresponds a right: we can have obligations towards certain men from whom we have nothing to expect, and also towards nature and animals, which do not owe us anything.[8]

In India, Hinduism represents the universe as a space where the beings traverse cycles of many forms of existence. In Taoism, the *tao* of the world is regarded as a universal fact that governs the course of beings and things. In Black Africa, the social relationship includes living beings as well as the dead. In the Middle East, the notions of respect and honour determine the obligations within the extended family and the clan.[9] All these facts are hardly reconcilable with the

---

7   S. S. Rama Rao Pappu, 'Human Rights and Human Obligations: An East-West Perspective', in *Philosophy and Social Action*, November/December 1982, p. 24.

8   Cf. Chung-Shu Lo, 'Human Rights in the Chinese Tradition', in UNESCO (ed.), *Human Rights: Comments and Interpretations — A Symposium* (London: Allan Wingate, 1950); John C. H. Wu, 'Chinese Legal and Political Philosophy', in Charles A. Moore (ed.), *The Chinese Mind* (Honolulu: University of Hawaii Press, 1967); and Joanne R. Bauer and Daniel A. Bell, *The East Asian Challenge for Human Rights* (Cambridge: Cambridge University Press, 1999).

9   Cf. David Little, John Kelsay and Abulaziz Sachedina, *Human Rights and the Conflicts of Culture: Western and Islamic Perspectives on Religious Liberty* (Columbia: University of South Carolina Press, 1988); and Ann Elizabeth Mayer, *Islam and Human Rights: Tradition and Politics*, 3rd rev. edition (Boulder: Westview Press, 1999).

theory of rights. 'Human rights are Western values', writes Sophia Mappa, 'which other societies, despite lip service, do not at all share'.[10]

To posit that what comes first is not the individual but the group does not at all signify that the individual is 'enclosed' in the group, but rather that he acquires his individuality only in connection with a social relationship which is also a constituent of his being. That does not signify either that the desire to escape despotism, coercion or ill treatment does not exist everywhere. Between the individual and the group, tensions may surge. That fact is indeed universal. But what is not at all universal is the belief according to which the best means of preserving freedom is to posit, in an abstract manner, an individual deprived of all his concrete characteristics, disconnected from all his natural and cultural affiliations. There are conflicts in all cultures, but in the majority of them, the vision of the world which predominates is not a conflicting vision (the individual against the group), but a 'cosmic' vision organised according to the order and the natural harmony of things. Each individual has his role to play in the whole into which he is positioned, and the role of political power is to ensure as best it can this coexistence and this harmony, which is the guarantee of eternity. Just as power is universal but the forms of power are not, the desire for freedom is universal, whereas the ways of responding to it can vary considerably.

The problem becomes especially acute when the social or cultural practices denounced in the name of human rights are not imposed practices but customary practices, evidently enjoying widespread popularity amidst given populations (which does not mean that they are never criticised by them). How can a doctrine founded on the free disposition of individuals by themselves oppose it? If the men should be left free to do what they want as long as the use of their freedom does not encroach upon that of the others, why could not peoples of whom certain customs appear to us shocking or condemnable be left free to practice them as long as they do not seek to impose them on others?

The classic example is that of female circumcision, still practiced today in numerous countries of Black Africa (as well as in certain Muslim countries). It is quite evidently a question of a harmful practice,

---

10 *Planetary Democracy: A Western Dream?* (London: IKO, 2001), p. 9. In the Third World, adds Sophia Mappa, the rejection of individualism illustrates the 'preference in many societies for polytheism and polygamy. The ideal, so dear to the West, of a single god and a unique love is hardly shared elsewhere' (*ibid.*, p. 18).

but it is difficult to extract it from an entire cultural and social context in which it is, on the contrary, considered as morally good and socially necessary: an uncircumcised woman will not be able to get married and will not be able to have children, which is why the women who are circumcised are the first to have their daughters circumcised. The question arises of determining in the name of what one can prohibit a custom which is not imposed on anybody. The only reasonable reply is that one can only provoke the people concerned to reflect on its favourableness, that is to say, to encourage an *internal* critique of the considered practice. It is those men and women whom the problem essentially concerns who should grapple with it.[11] To cite another example, when a woman is stoned in a Muslim country and that infuriates the defenders of human rights, one can ask oneself exactly what this condemnation relates to: to the mode of execution (stoning), to the fact that adultery should be punished by death (or that it is quite simply punishable), or to the death penalty itself? The first reason seems of a mostly emotional sort.[12] The second can at least be discussed (whatever feeling one may have on the question, in the name of what can one prevent the members of a given culture from considering adultery to be an offense that merits sanction and from freely evaluating the gravity of this punishment?). As for the third, it makes of every country that maintains the death penalty, beginning with the United States, a violator of human rights.

'To pretend to attribute a universal validity to human rights formulated in this way', writes Raimundo Panikkar, 'is to postulate that the majority of the peoples of the world are engaged, practically in the same way as the Western nations, in a process of transition from a more or less mythical *Gemeinschaft*[13] ... to a 'modernity' organised in a 'rational' and 'contractual' manner, such as the industrial Western

---

11 One will note that female circumcision is not practised either in the African population of the West Indies nor among the American negroes. In the United States, sexual mutilations (circumcision) are exclusively restricted to men.

12 The stoning of an adulterous woman is not a specifically Muslim practice. In the past it was habitually practised in Israel (*Leviticus* 20:10; *Deuteronomy* 22:22-24), including during the epoch of Jesus (*John* 8:3-6).

13 German: 'community'. The German sociologist Ferdinand Tönnies first coined the term to designate a group in which the individuals within it are more concerned with the good of the whole as opposed to their own welfare, including in terms of values.-Ed.

world knows it. That is a contestable postulate'.[14] So much so that 'to proclaim the concept of human rights ... could well be shown to be a Trojan horse introduced secretly into the heart of other civilisations with the aim of forcing them to accept those modes of existence, thought and feeling for which human rights constitute an emergency solution'.[15]

To accept cultural diversity demands a full recognition of the Other. But how to recognise the Other if his values and practices are opposed to those that one wishes to inculcate? The adherents of the ideology of rights are generally partisans of 'pluralism'. But what compatibility is there between human rights and the plurality of cultural systems and religious beliefs? If the respect for individual rights passes through a non-respect for cultures and peoples, should one conclude from this that all men are equal, but that the cultures that these equals have created are not equal?

The imposition of human rights represents, quite evidently, an acculturation whose realisation risks bringing about the dislocation or eradication of collective identities which also play a role in the constitution of individual identities. The Classical idea according to which human rights protect the individuals against the groups to which they belong and constitute a recourse with regard to the practices, laws and customs that characterise these groups thereby proves to be doubtful. Do those who denounce such or such a 'violation of human rights' always measure exactly at what point the practice that they criticise can be characteristic of the culture in the midst of which it is observed? Are those who complain of the violation of their rights ready, for their part, to pay for the observation of these rights with the destruction of their culture? Would they not rather wish that their rights be recognised on the basis of what specifies their culture?

'Individuals', writes Paul Piccone, 'are protected only when the essence of human rights is already embedded in a community's particular legal system and the people really believe in them.'[16] This remark is correct. By definition, human rights can be invoked only where they are already recognised, in the cultures and countries which

---

14 *Art. cit.*, p. 98.

15 *Ibid.*, p. 100.

16 'Ten Counter-Theses on New Class Ideology: Yet Another Reply to Rich Johnstone', in *Telos* 119, Spring 2001, p. 146.

have already internalised their principles — that is to say, where, theoretically, one should no longer have any need of invoking them. But if human rights can only be efficacious where the principles on which they are founded have already been internalised, the dislocation of cultures provoked by their brutal importation goes directly against the objective being pursued. 'The paradox of human rights', adds Piccone, 'is that their implementation implies the erosion and destruction of the conditions (traditions and customs) without which their implementation becomes precisely impossible'.[17]

*

It was to try to reconcile the ideology of rights with cultural diversity that the notion of the rights of peoples to self-determination was elaborated. This new category of rights was theorised in particular immediately after the Second World War, notably in the context of the nationalistic demands that were to end in decolonisation, but also under the influence of ethnological works such as Claude Lévi-Strauss'[18] which, in reaction to the adherents of social evolutionism (Lewis Morgan),[19] denounced the ravages of acculturation and placed

---

17 *Ibid.*, p. 150.

18 Claude Lévi-Strauss (1908-2009) is regarded as one of the most important anthropologists of the Twentieth century. In his book *Race and History* (Paris: UNESCO, 1952), p. 12, he wrote, '[T]he strength and the weakness of the great declarations of human rights has always been that, in proclaiming an ideal, they too often forget that man grows to man's estate surrounded, not by humanity in the abstract, but by a traditional culture, where even the most revolutionary changes leave whole sectors quite unaltered. Such declarations can themselves be accounted for by the situation existing at a particular moment in time and in particular space. Faced with the two temptations of condemning things which are offensive to him emotionally or of denying differences which are beyond his intellectual grasp, modern man has launched out on countless lines of philosophical and sociological speculation in a vain attempt to achieve a compromise between these two contradictory poles, and to account for the diversity of cultures while seeking, at the same time, to eradicate what still shocks and offends him in that diversity'.-Ed.

19 Lewis Henry Morgan (1818-1881) was an American lawyer who also conducted research into ethnology. He became fascinated with the Native Americans and was initiated into the Iroquois tribe. In his book *Systems of Consanguinity and Affinity of the Human Family*, he compared his studies of the Native Americans with the tribal life of other cultures, and developed his theory of the Unity of Origin of

the accent on cultural specificities or on the need of recognising rights particular to ethnic minorities. More recently, the renewal of identitarian affirmations of all sorts, a compensatory reaction during the decline of national identities and the growing sclerosis of nation-states has set this subject once again as the order of the day. For Lelio Basso,[20] a great defender of the rights of peoples to self-determination, the true 'subjects of history are the peoples, who are equally the subjects of right.'[21]

A Universal Declaration of the Rights of Peoples was adopted in Algeria on 4 July 1976, the anniversary of the bicentenary of the American Declaration of Independence. It stipulates that 'every people has the right to respect its national and cultural identity' (Article 2), that every people 'determine its political status in total freedom' (Article 5), that it possesses 'an exclusive right to its riches and natural resources' (Article 8), that it has the 'right to give itself the economic and social system of its choice' (Article 11), the 'right to speak its language, to preserve and to develop its culture' (Article 13), as well as 'the right not to see a culture imposed on it which is alien to it.'[22]

The enumeration of these rights alone, which for the most part have remained a dead letter, suffices to show to what point their harmonisation with the Classical theory of human rights is problematic.

Mankind, in which he believed he had identified the universal primordial social structure of humanity. He also came to believe in the necessity for continual progress in societies in order for them to survive, which he identified in modern times with technological progress, as described in his *Ancient Society*. Marx and Engels were heavily reliant on Morgan's work when discussing tribal societies and social progress in their own theories.-Ed.

20 Leilo Basso (1903-1978) was an Italian lawyer and a socialist politician who opposed the Fascists. During the 1960s he participated in the Russell Tribunal, founded by the philosopher Bertrand Russell, to examine American war crimes in Vietnam. During the 1970s he also investigated abuses by Latin American regimes and established several organisations which supported national liberation movements.-Ed.

21 Cited by Edmond Jouve, *Le droit des peuples* (Paris: PUF, 1986), p. 7.

22 A 'Green' Declaration of Human Rights, patronised by Colonel al-Qadhafi, was likewise adopted in Libya on 14 May 1977. An African Charter of Human Rights and Peoples' Rights was adopted on 28 June 1981 at the Nairobi summit of the Organisation of African Unity. A Universal Islamic Declaration of Human Rights was proclaimed some months later, on 19 September 1981, in the offices of UNESCO. It is founded on the *Qur'an* and notably affirms the right to religious freedom (Article 13).

The right to maintain a collective identity, for example, can antagonise certain individual rights. The right to collective security can also bring about severe limitations of individual freedoms. In a more general way, writes Norbert Rouland, 'it is certain that the notion of human rights has the effect of blocking the recognition of the collective rights of ethnic groups'.[23] As for the rights of peoples to organise themselves, which has served as the basis of decolonisation, it contradicts straightaway the right to interference with a 'humanitarian' objective.[24]

The optimists think that the individual rights and collective rights are spontaneously harmonised because they are complementary, although opinions differ on the hierarchy that is imposed between the former and the latter. Edmond Jouve thus assures us that 'human rights and the rights of peoples to self-determination cannot contradict each other'.[25] Others, more numerous, stress undeniable contradictions, but draw opposite conclusions from them. 'Many of them have come to think that the notion of the rights of peoples to self-determination was only an abstraction destined to justify the replacement of one oppression by another and that only the rights of individuals counted', observes Léo Matarasso. 'Others, on the contrary, consider that human rights are only invoked as an ideological alibi to justify actions prejudicial to the rights of peoples to self-determination'.[26]

One finds the same diversity of opinions with regard to the 'universal', or, on the contrary, strictly Western, character of human rights.

---

23 'Anthropologie juridique: aux confins du droit', in *Sciences humaines*, May 1992, p. 33.

24 The question of the right of peoples to self-determination comes up against a classical difficulty: the definition of the people in international law and its legal distinction in relation to the state, indispensable if one wishes to defend the rights of minorities. Cf. on this subject Alain Fenet (ed.), *Droits de l'homme, droits des peuples* (Paris: PUF, 1982).

25 *Op. cit.*, p. 108.

26 Jacques Julliard has gone so far as to write that 'the rights of peoples to self-determination has become the principal instrument of the strangling of human rights' (*Le Tiers-monde et la gauche* [Paris: Seuil, 1979], p. 38). The right to difference is equally condemned by a determined partisan of acculturation, Sélim Abou, who, in *Culture et droits de l'homme* (Paris: Hachette-Pluriel, 1992), violently attacks Lévi-Strauss. The same author assures us that 'human rights find their foundation in the rational nature of man, insofar as reason is the demand of freedom for oneself and for others and that this demand constitutes a natural inalienable right' (p. 75).

Following Alain Renaut, who affirms that 'the reference to universal values does not in no way implies contempt for the individual',[27] a majority of the partisans of the ideology of rights continue to force-fully maintain its universality. 'Human rights', declares John Rawls, 'are not the consequence of a particular philosophy, nor of one way among others of looking at the world. They are not tied to the cultural tradition of the West alone, even if it was within this tradition that they were formulated for the first time. They just follow from the definition of justice'.[28] The implicit postulate here is evidently that there is only one possible definition of justice. [T]hough it is true that the values implicit in the Universal Declaration of Human Rights derive from the Enlightenment tradition, virtually every country in the world has affirmed them'.[29] How is it, then, that it is necessary to have recourse to arms so often in order to impose them?

From such a perspective, it would be in some way by chance that the West had arrived earlier than the others at the 'stage' where it would have been possible to explicitly formulates an aspiration present everywhere in a latent way. This historical priority would not confer on it a particular moral superiority. The Westerners would be just 'in advance', whereas the other cultures would be 'behind'. That is the classical scheme of the ideology of progress.

The discussion of the universality of human rights, in fact, evokes very often those 'ecumenical' dialogues where one wrongly takes for granted that all the religious beliefs echo, in different forms, common 'truths'. The reasoning maintained to demonstrate that the rights are universal is almost always the same. It consists of affirming that there exists everywhere in the world a desire for well-being and freedom, and then of deriving a ground from which to legitimate that discourse of rights which is considered to be a response to this demand.[30] Now, such a conclusion is perfectly erroneous. Nobody has ever denied that all men have certain aspirations in common, nor that a consensus may be established to consider at least certain things as intrinsically good

---

27 'Droits de l'homme', in *L'Express*, 30 September 1988, p. 55.

28 *Le Monde*, 30 November 1993, p. 2.

29 'Power, Principles and Human Rights', in *The National Interest*, Summer 2002, p. 117.

30 Cf. for example Michael J. Perry, 'Are Human Rights Universal? The Relativist Challenge and Related Matters', in *Human Rights Quarterly*, August 1997, pp. 461-509.

or intrinsically bad. Everywhere in the world men prefer to be healthy rather than ill, free rather than restricted, everywhere they hate to be beaten, tortured, imprisoned arbitrarily, massacred, etc. But from the fact that certain conditions are human, it does not follow at all that the discourse of rights is validated, and much less that it is universal. In other words, it is not the universality of the desire to escape coercion that it is a question of demonstrating, but the universality of the language that one expects to use to respond to this desire. The two levels cannot be confused. And the second demonstration has still not been achieved.The way in which the different values are combined among themselves is, besides, rarely abstract in the majority of cultures, for the simple reason that each of these values receives a different complexion within each culture. As Charles Taylor has emphasised several times, to say that a value is good is the same, at first, as saying that that culture in which this value is favoured itself deserves to be considered good. As for reason, which is far from being axiologically neutral, every attempt at associating it with any value, even one which is decreed to be 'universal', ties it inexorably to the particular culture where this value is honoured.

To the question, 'Is the concept of human rights a universal concept?', Raimundo Panikkar responds thus with clarity: 'The reply is quite simply no, and that for three reasons. A) No concept is universal in itself. Each concept is valid in the first place where it has been conceived. If we wish to extend its validity beyond the limits of its proper context, we should justify this extrapolation... Besides, every concept tends to univocity.[31] To accept the possibility of universal concepts would imply a strictly rationalist conception of truth. But even if this position corresponded to the theoretical truth, the existence of universal concepts would not result from it, on account of the plurality of the universe of discourse which mankind *de facto* presents... B) Amidst the vast field of Western culture itself, even the postulates that serve to locate our problem are not universally admitted. C) If one would just adopt the attitude of a transcultural mind, the problem would appear exclusively Western, that is to say, it is the question itself that is in

---

31 Univocity is that which speaks with one voice. In philosophy, it implies a concept, such as goodness, which is the same everywhere, and varies only in terms of degree.-Ed.

question. The majority of the postulates and other related presuppositions enumerated above are quite simply absent from other cultures'.[32]

This is the reason why certain authors have resigned themselves
to admitting that human rights are a 'Western construct with limited applicability',[33] applicable with difficulty in any case in the cultures whose tradition is alien to liberal individualism. Raymond Aron
had himself recognised it: 'Every declaration of rights would appear
finally as the idealised expression of the political or social order that a
certain class or a certain civilisation is forced to realise... By the same
token, one understands the equivocality of the Universal Declaration
of Rights of 1948. It borrows from Western civilisation even the practice of a declaration of rights, since other civilisations are unaware not
of collective norms or individual rights, but of the theoretical expression, claiming to be universal, of the former or of the latter'.[34]

The critique of the universalism of rights in the name of cultural
pluralism is not new. Herder[35] and Savigny,[36] in Germany, like Henry
Sumner Maine[37] in England, have shown that legal matters could not
be understood without taking into account the cultural variables. One
finds an analogous critique in Hannah Arendt[38] when she writes that

---

32 *Art. cit.*, pp. 94-96.

33 Adamantia Pollis and Peter Schwab, *art. cit.*

34 'Pensée sociologique et droits de l'homme', in *Etudes politiques* (Paris: Gallimard,
    1972), p. 232.

35 Johann Gottfried Herder (1744-1803) was a German philosopher who
    emphasised the importance of linguistic and geographical differences giving rise
    to unique identities among nations, thus stressing subjectivity over universality in
    history.-Ed.

36 Friedrich Carl von Savigny (1779-1861) was a German jurist who believed that
    law is something that can only be derived from the specific culture and history of
    a nation, and not something that can be universally applied to all nations, as was
    held by the French jurists of his day.-Ed.

37 Sir Henry Sumner Maine (1822-1888) was an English jurist and historian. Initially
    a student of ancient Roman law, he compared the Roman concept of the individual
    as someone whose identity was bound to his identity in specific traditional groups
    to the modern concept of the autonomous individual. After spending many
    years in India, Maine concluded that there is no single system of law that can be
    universally applied, and also that democracy was not inherently superior to other
    political systems.-Ed.

38 Hannah Arendt (1906-1975) was a German-Jewish political theorist who studied
    with Martin Heidegger. She fled the Nazis and lived for most of the remainder

'the paradox of abstract rights is that in deriving the rights from a displaced humanity, they risk depriving of identity those who are precisely victims of the deracinations imposed by modern conflicts'.

On the same grounds, Alasdair MacIntyre addresses three objections to the ideology of human rights. The first is that the notion of rights, such as this ideology posits it, is not found everywhere, which shows that it is not intrinsically necessary to social life. The second is that the discussion of rights, even when it professes to proclaim rights derived from an atemporal human nature, is narrowly circumscribed to a determined historical period, which renders the universality of its discourse hardly credible. The third is that every attempt to justify the belief in such rights ends in failure. Emphasising that one can only have rights and enjoy them in a type of society possessing certain established rules, MacIntyre writes: 'These rules appear only in particular historical periods and in particular social circumstances. These are not at all universal characteristics of the human condition.'[39] He concludes from this that such rights are, just like sorcerers and unicorns, only a fiction.[40]

*

The theory of human rights, insofar as it is posited straightaway as a universal truth, represents in certain respects a reaction against relativism. There is a certain paradox there, since this theory emanates from the same doctrinal liberalism which, historically, has also legitimised relativism by proclaiming the equal right of each individual to pursue the ends that he has independently chosen. (The contradiction appears clearly in those who praise 'multiculturalism' from a strictly relativist position, when they denounce at the same time such or such a cultural tradition as an 'attack on human rights'.) But the ideology of human rights, if it avoids relativism, inversely runs the risk of falling into ethnocentrism. This is what Hubert Védrine, the former Minister

---

of her life in the United States, becoming one of the most influential political philosophers of the Twentieth century.-Ed.

39 *Op. cit.*, p. 68.

40 *Ibid.*, p. 70.

of Foreign Affairs,[41] confirmed when he said that the bible of human rights comes to consider 'that Western values are, *en masse* and without possible discussion or nuance, universal and invariable values and that every questioning on this subject, every pragmatism is a sacrilege'.[42]

'To hold as established that, without an explicit recognition of human rights, life would be chaotic and deprived of meaning', writes Raimundo Panikkar for his part, 'derives from the same mentality as maintaining that, without the belief in a sole God such as is understood in the Abrahamic tradition, human life would be dissolved into total anarchy. It would suffice to push a little further in this direction to conclude that atheists, Buddhists and animists, for example, must be considered as the representations of human aberrations. In the same vein: either human rights or chaos'.[43]

Such a slide is avoidable only with difficulty. As soon as a doctrine or a culture believes that it is the bearer of a 'universal' message it manifests an invincible propensity to travesty its particular values as such. It then disqualifies the values of others, which it perceives as deceptive, irrational, imperfect or quite simply outmoded. With the best of good intentions, since it is convinced that it speaks in the name of truth, it professes intolerance. 'A universalist doctrine evolves ineluctably toward a model equivalent to the one-party state', said Lévi-Strauss.[44]

In an epoch when cultural and human diversity is indeed the last thing about which the economic and market ideology that dominates the planet is concerned, the ideology of rights thus surreptitiously resumes old discussions of domination and acculturation. Accompanying the planetary extension of the market, it provides it with the 'humanitarian' dress which it needs. It is no longer in the name of the 'true faith', of 'civilisation', of 'progress', or indeed of the 'White man's burden'[45] that the West believes that it is justified in directing the

---

41 Hubert Védrine (b. 1947) was the Foreign Minister in Prime Minister Jospin's Socialist administration between 1997 and 2002. Védrine is well-known for his opposition to American hegemony and popularised the term 'hyperpower' to describe America's position in world affairs.-Ed.

42 'Refonder la politique étrangère française', in *Le Monde diplomatique*, December 2000, p. 3.

43 *Art. cit.*, p. 97.

44 *The View from Afar* (New York: Basic Books, 1985), p. 285.

45 'I do not adopt without reserve the French ideology of "right of interference"', said Hubert Védrine as well. 'First, because it resembles too much indeed the "duty of

social and cultural practices existing in the world, but in the name of the morality incarnated in the law. The affirmation of the universality of human rights, in this sense, does not represent anything else but the conviction that particular values, those of modern Western civilisation, are superior values which must be imposed everywhere. The discussion of rights permits the West once more to install itself as the moral judge of humankind.

'In identifying the defence of human rights and the defence of Western values', write René Gallissot and Michel Trebitsch, 'a new, more insidious and more subtle ideology, a "soft" ideology allows one to substitute for the East-West Manichaeism born in the Cold War, a North-South Manichaeism where Western-style freedom hopes to regain its virginity'.[46] 'The Western model', observes, for her part, Sophia Mappa, '...must be imposed on humanity as if it were endowed with a natural objectivity which would ensure it superiority over the others. According to the same idea, the diverse social systems of the globe would be variants of the Western system, whose specificities should disappear before the irresistible advance of the latter on the planetary level... In order that the Western system may win the planet, it would [therefore] be necessary that the other societies consciously abandon deeply rooted representations of the world, values, social practices, cultural institutions and symbols'.[47]

Could it have gone otherwise? One may seriously doubt it. As François Flahaut writes, 'If the Western world wishes to convince the planet of the validity of human rights such as it has conceived them, it should assume the anthropological and theological presuppositions which support its formulations (and notably the specific use of the term "rights" in the expression "human rights"). If, on the other hand, it wishes to avoid supporting itself on these presuppositions, then it should recognise that the formulation that it has given of these "rights" draws from its own tradition and has a universal value only to the degree to which it appeals to a moral sentiment shared by all men of

---

civilisation" of the French colonialists of the Nineteenth century and the White man's burden of Rudyard Kipling' (*art. cit.*, p. 3).

46 *Les droits de l'homme et le nouvel occidentalisme*, special issue of *L'Homme et la société*, Paris, 1987, 3-4, p. 7. Cf. also Rino Genovese, *La tribù occidentale* (Turin: Bollati Boringhieri, 1995).

47 *Op. cit.*, pp. 9-10.

good will.'[48] 'In a general way', said Raymond Aron, 'one could pose the following dilemma: either the rights attain a certain sort of universality because they tolerate, thanks to the vagueness of the conceptual formulation, no matter what institution; or they preserve some precision and lose their value of universality'.[49] And, to conclude: 'The rights called universal merit this qualification only on the condition of being formulated in a language so vague that they lose all definite content'.[50]

François de Smet summarises the same dilemma in these terms: 'Either we decide on a lax, empty international law that is flexible at will since it respects the conceptions of all the human cultures, and therefore probably ineffective; or we assume a position according to which our culture, that of individual rights, of the value of the individual *vis-à-vis* the collectivity, is superior to the others, a superiority which is often affirmed arbitrarily, for we assume such a moral predominance thanks to our own premises'.[51]

To contest the universality of the theory of rights does not, however, mean that it is necessary to approve no matter what political, cultural or social practice for the sole reason that it exists. To recognise the free capacity of peoples and cultures to give themselves, by and for themselves, laws that they wish to adopt, or to conserve the customs and practices which are theirs, does not automatically bring about their approval. The freedom of judgment remains, it is only the conclusion that one draws from it that can vary. The misuse that an individual or a group makes of its freedom leads to the condemnation of this use, not of this freedom.

It is thus not at all a question of adopting a relativist position — which is an untenable position — but rather of a pluralist position. There exists a plurality of cultures and these cultures respond differently to the aspirations that are expressed therein. Certain of these responses can rightly appear to us contestable. It is perfectly normal to condemn them — and to refuse to adopt them ourselves. One should admit also that a society can evolve in a direction that we consider to be preferable

---

48 *Le sentiment d'exister: Ce soi qui ne va pas de soi* (Paris: Descartes et Cie, 2002), pp. 454-455.

49 *Op. cit.*, p. 228.

50 *Ibid.*, p. 232.

51 *Les droits de l'homme: Origines et aléas d'une idéologie moderne* (Paris: Cerf, 2001), p. 140.

only from cultural realities and social practices that are its own. These replies can also be seen to be contradictory. One should then recognise that there does not exist any overarching example from a superior, all-encompassing point of view which would allow us to resolve these contradictions.

Raimundo Panikkar has, besides, shown very well that one can find in all cultures without difficulty 'anthropomorphic equivalents' of the concept of human rights, but that these equivalents — in India the notion of *dharma*, in China the notion of *li* (rite) — are neither 'translations' nor synonyms, nor even antitheses, but only ways of replying to an equivalent need proper to each culture.

When Joseph de Maistre,[52] in a passage that has often been cited, says that he has met in his life all sorts of men, but that he has never seen man himself, he does not deny the existence of a human nature.[53] He only affirms that there does not exist any example where this nature can be apprehended in a pure state, independently of all particular context: the fact of belonging to humanity is always mediated by a culture or a collectivity. It would therefore be an error to conclude from this that human nature does not exist: that the objective reality is indissociable from a context or an interpretation does not mean that it is reduced to this context, that it is nothing other than this interpretation. 'There exists a right that is natural', emphasises Eric Weil, '...but it is different everywhere. Different everywhere: it is not the same in a traditional community, in a political organisation of a tyrannical type, in the state of a modern society. To conclude from this that such a nature exists only among us would be absurd, just as absurd as it would be to affirm that the problem of a right that is natural has been, can have been, or should have been posited everywhere.'[54]

---

52 Joseph de Maistre (1753-1821) was a French Counter-Enlightenment philosopher who fled the Revolution and lived the remainder of his life in Italy. He always remained a staunch opponent of democracy and supported monarchical rule.-Ed.

53 'During my life, I have seen Frenchmen, Italians, Russians, and so on; thanks to Montesquieu, I even know that one can be *Persian*; but I must say, as for *man*, I have never come across him anywhere.' From Marc A. Goldstein, *Social and Political Thought of the French Revolution, 1788-1797* (New York: Peter Lang, 1997), p. 820.-Ed.

54 'Du droit naturel', in *Essais et conférences* (Paris: Plon, 1970), p. 193.

In *Fragile humanité*,[55] Myriam Revault d'Allones has proposed an interesting phenomenology of the human fact, not in the sense of a construction of others through the sphere of subjectivity, but in a relational perspective which posits above all the 'significance of the human' as a capacity for exchanging experiences. Humanity, she says, is not a functional category, but a 'disposition to inhabit and to share the world'.[56] One can draw from this the conclusion that humanity does not yield itself as a unitary fact but on a basis of common sharing.

---

55 Paris: Aubier, 2002.
56 *Ibid.*, p. 37.

IV

BEYOND HUMAN RIGHTS: POLITICS, FREEDOM, DEMOCRACY

From Augustin Cochin[1] to Joseph de Maistre, from Edmund Burke[2] to Karl Marx, from Hannah Arendt to Michel Villey, the majority of the critiques of the ideology of human rights have denounced its universalism and abstract egalitarianism. They have equally called attention to the fact that, in depriving all concrete characteristics from man, whose rights they proclaim, of this ideology, they have risked ending in levelling and uniformisation. If one admits that the affirmation of human rights essentially aims at guaranteeing the autonomy of individuals, one understands at the same time that there is a contradiction there.

The abstraction of human rights is what threatens most to render them inoperative. The principal reason for this is that it is contradictory to affirm, at the same time, the absolute value of the individual and the equality of individuals in the sense of a fundamental identity. If all men are equal, if they are all fundamentally the same, if they are all 'men like others', far from the unique personality of each of them being able to be recognised, they will appear, not as irreplaceable, but on the contrary as interchangeable. Not being different from

---

1 Augustin Cochin (1876-1916) was a historian who sought to analyse the French Revolution from a sociological perspective. He was killed in action in the First World War.-Ed.

2 Edmund Burke (1729-1797) was an Irish politician and philosopher who sat in the House of Commons as a member of the Whig party. He was opposed to democracy and the French Revolution, although he did believe in the importance of representative government and supported the cause of the American Revolution. He was also involved for many years in addressing injustices perpetrated by the British East India Company in India.-Ed.

one another by their particular qualities, only their more or less great number will make a difference. Abstract equivalence, in other words, necessarily contradicts the proclamation of the absolute individuality of the subjects: no man can be at the same time 'unique' and basically identical to every other. Inversely, one cannot affirm the unique value of an individual even while considering his personal characteristics as indifferent, that is to say, without specifying what makes him different from the others. A world where all are equal is not a world where 'nothing is worth a life'[3] but a world where a life is worth nothing.

This problem had been glimpsed by Alexis de Tocqueville,[4] who related the rise in the value of equality to the risk of uniformisation at the core of social life.[5] It has been repeated more recently by Hannah Arendt, who shows that to posit man as a pure abstraction is to increase his vulnerability. 'The conception of human rights, based upon the assumed existence of a human being as such, broke down at the very moment when those who professed to believe in it were for the first time confronted with people who had indeed lost all other qualities and specific relationships — except that they were still human. The world found nothing sacred in the abstract nakedness of being human.'[6]

Summarising the thesis of Hannah Arendt, André Clair underlines the 'relation between the affirmation of abstract universal rights and the failure of human rights in ensuring the most elementary respect

---

3   This is a famous quote from André Malraux's novel The Conquerors (Chicago: University of Chicago Press, 1992), p. 155. The full quote reads, 'I've also learned that a life isn't worth anything, but nothing is worth a life.'-Ed.

4   Alexis De Tocqueville (1805-1859) was a French political thinker best known for his work, *Democracy in America*, which was based on his experiences while travelling in the U.S. Although De Tocqueville was a democrat who opposed the monarchy of his day, he also opposed the socialist radicals. In his study of the U.S., he praised America's democratic system, but disliked Americans' obsession with money and their contempt for elites, since even though the latter is what enabled them to do away with the old colonial aristocracy, it also caused them to disregard the most intelligent members of their society, coining the term 'tyranny of the majority' to describe it.-Ed.

5   Cf. *Democracy in America* (New York: Library of America, 2004), vol. 4, chapter 6, pp. 816-821.

6   *The Origins of Totalitarianism* (Orlando: Harcourt Brace Jovanovich, 1976), p. 299. In this work, Hannah Arendt ties her critique of the theory of human rights to a denunciation of totalitarianism, itself present as social atomisation and forced equalisation of all individuals.

for human beings as persons. Precisely what the doctrine of human rights fails to recognise, with its thesis of abstract equality, is that there are no effective rights without a recognition of the differences between beings. That is the point of the thesis: human rights can only be rights of *individuality*... Of course, there follows a relativity of rights linked to their efficiency, that of a historical community. But much more than that, it is a question of a metaphysical thesis, that of ontological difference: the law does not have its principle in man, not even in a fundamental universal subjectivity, but it is an element of the world; it is the ontological difference, unrecognised by the affirmation of abstract equality, that alone gives its full significance to human rights, in recognising first a superiority in a world already constituted of meanings... It is not at all a question of an absolute right of everybody to difference, but of recognising that only rights rooted in traditions and community experiences have efficacy'.[7]

It is only too easy to recall here that the same that has affirmed the rights of individuals most strongly is also that which, in fact, has put in place the most weighty mechanisms of collective heteronomy. The two phenomena, one knows today, had to go together, even if that were only because the state alone, having rapidly become a welfare state, was able to attenuate the destructive effects of the rise in individualism on the social fabric. Now, the intervention of the state in all fields contradicts the autonomy of wills that is considered to be the basis of the responsibility of the subjects of the law.

'The emancipation of individuals from the primordial restraint which committed them to a community which it is claimed preceded them as regards its ordering principle, and which profited from very effective hierarchical links between man and man', observes Marcel Gauchet, 'far from entailing a reduction of the role of authority, as common sense would suggest through simple deduction, has constantly contributed to enlarge it. The undeniable latitude acquired by individual agents at all levels has not at all prevented, but on the contrary, has regularly favoured the constitution, above and beyond the sphere of civil autonomy, of an administrative apparatus taking over

---

7   *Droit, communauté et humanité* (Paris: Cerf, 2000), pp. 92-93. The abstract character of the formula is especially marked in French (*droits de l'homme*), less in German, which speaks of 'rights of men' (*Menschenrechte*), and still less in English, Spanish or Italian, which use an adjective instead of a noun (human rights, *derechos humanos*, *diritti umani*).

more and more broadly and minutely the collective direction... The deeper the laws of men enter into the definition of their society, the more the organisational dominance of the bureaucratic state, under cover of permitting their participation in it, robs them, in fact, of this faculty'.[8] What remains then, today, of the 'reign of human rights'? In contemporary life, the question of foundations is, for all intents and purposes, no longer posed. Our contemporaries no longer base these rights on human nature, since the time they have known that no 'state of nature' ever preceded life in society, and especially since the time they learned that 'nature', insofar as it has something to tell us, goes in a very different direction from that of the ideology of rights. But, for all that, they have not become Kantian. They seek rather to conserve the notion of 'dignity' even while detaching it from all notion of a moral law. 'To respect the dignity of another human being', observes Pierre Manent, 'is no longer to respect the respect which he conserves in himself for the moral law; it is today, more and more, to respect the choice that he has made, whatever this choice may be, in the realisation of his rights'.

The present tendency, more precisely, consists in converting all sorts of demands, desires or interests into 'rights'. Individuals, in the extreme case, would have the 'right' to see no matter what demand satisfied, for the sole reason that they can formulate them. Today, to claim rights is only a way of seeking to maximise one's interest. The future of the consumer of rights thus converges with the economic ideal of man solely preoccupied with augmenting his utility. 'The *Homo oeconomicus* in search of his interest', remarks Guy Roustang, 'has his homologue in the world of politics: the individual who is defined by his rights'.[9] That is why the citizen has increasingly more difficulty in finding his place in a society that is politically conceived on the model of a self-regulated market. Reduced to a simple catalogue of desires posed as so many needs, rights thus continually proliferate without any longer encumbering themselves with a true *raison d'être*. This inflation of rights corresponds to what Michael J. Sandel has called

---

8   *La démocratie contre elle-même* (Paris: Gallimard-Tel, 2002), pp. 20-21.

9   *Démocratie: le risque du marché* (Paris: Desclée de Brouwer, 2002), p. 176.

the 'procedural republic'[10] and to the consecration of the idol of the 'dependent individualist' (Fred Siegel).[11]

Is one then still in a society which 'respects human rights' or in a society which has decided to legitimise all the forms of desire, to 'recognise' all the choices of life, all the contents of existence, all the preferences and all the orientations, provided that these do not interfere too much with those of one's neighbours? Does recognising human rights lead to considering all tendencies as legitimate?

In any case, the banalisation of rights brings about their devaluation. 'This pluralism without limits', writes Simone Goyard-Fabre, 'engenders a tragic dereliction: a legal dereliction, since the concept of right is dissolved in the uncontrolled movement of demands without end; an ontological dereliction, for the fact that the human being declines his personal responsibility in order to gain the advantage of a responsibility claimed to be collective engenders irresponsibility...; an axiological dereliction, for the total permissiveness which is at the horizon of the delirious overproduction of rights contains the beginnings of a passage to extremes where immoderation and excess bear forces similar to those of a nihilist flood'.[12]

Another result, directly related to the affirmation of the individual and his rights, is the extraordinary rise in power of the legal sphere, henceforth perceived as capable of regulating political life and of pacifying social life by itself. Tocqueville said that, in the United States, there is hardly a political question that does not end by turning itself sooner or later into a legal question. This situation has slowly extended to all the Western countries, where the powers of the judges do not cease expand and where social relations are increasingly determined

---

10 Sandel first coined this term in his article, 'The Political Theory of the Procedural Republic', Revue de metaphysique et de morale 93, January/March 1988, p. 61, and in his book *Liberalism and the Limits of Justice* (Cambridge: Cambridge University Press, 1982).-Ed.

11 On the inflation of rights, cf. F. Ost and M. Van de Kerchove, *Le système juridique entre ordre et désordre* (Paris: PUF, 1988); and Stamatios Tzitzis, 'Droits de l'homme et droit humanitaire', in Henri Pallard and Stamatios Tzitzis (eds.), *Droits fondamentaux et spécificités culturelles* (Paris: L'Harmattan, 1997), pp. 41-62. (Fred Siegel, a senior fellow at the Progressive Policy Institute and a former advisor to Mayor Rudolph Giuliani, discusses dependent individualism in *The Future Once Happened Here: New York, DC, LA, and the Fate of America's Big Cities* [New York: Free Press, 1997]).

12 *Les principes philosophiques du droit politique moderne* (Paris: PUF, 1997), p. 274.

in terms of rights. 'As a result, the realm of politics becomes merely the terrain where individuals...understood as rational agents in search of self-advantage — within the constraints of morality, of course — submit to procedures for adjudicating between their claims that they consider "fair".'[13]

The problem is that the declarations of rights, to the extent that they wish to encompass everything, are inevitably vaguer than the national laws. The difficulty, then, is to translate them into a positive right, without reducing the consensus of which they are the object. This is the source of paradox, well raised by Pierre Manent: 'In the future, if one depends principally upon human rights to render justice, the 'manner of judging' will be irreparable. Arbitrariness, that is to say precisely what our regimes wanted to defend themselves against in instituting the authority of constitutionality, will then go on increasing, and will paradoxically become the work of the judges. Now, a power which discovers that it can act arbitrarily will not delay in using and abusing this latitude. It tends towards despotism'.[14]

The international law issued by the Peace of Westphalia (1648)[15] is today equally turned upside down by the ideology of human rights, which justifies the right (or the duty) of 'humanitarian interference', that is to say, preventive war, formerly seen as nearly identical to a war of aggression. This right of humanitarian interference, which patently violates the Charter of the United Nations, has no precedent in international law.[16] It suggests that every state, whatever it be, can intervene at will in the internal affairs of another state, whatever it be, under the pretext of preventing 'attacks on human rights'. Justifying politico-military intervention, which decolonisation had theoretically put to

---

13 Chantal Mouffe, *The Return of the Political* (London: Verso, 1993), p. 140.

14 *Art. cit.*, p. 502.

15 The Thirty Years' War ended with the Peace of Westphalia in 1648, in which the nations of Europe recognised each others' territorial integrity. Some historians consider it to have been the first step in the development of the modern-day system of international relations.-Ed.

16 It was nevertheless prepared by the slow evolution of international law which, at least since the Treaty of Versailles (1919), has moved increasingly farther away from the ancient *jus publicum europaeum*. Already in 1917, the American President Woodrow Wilson had introduced into international law a discriminatory conception of war which makes the 'just war' the equivalent of a crusade. On this vast subject, cf. Carl Schmitt, *The* Nomos *of the Earth in the International Law of the* Jus Publicum Europaeum (New York: Telos Press, 2003).

an end, it permits a group of countries or authorities professing to act in the name of a nebulous 'international community' to impose their viewpoint everywhere without taking into account either cultural preferences or political and social practices accepted or ratified democratically. One immediately sees the risks of deviation related to such a doctrine, which quite simply opens the gate to wars without end, the *jus ad bellum* replacing the *jus in bello*.[17]

The idea of a justice being exercised beyond one's borders can certainly seduce. It is necessary to see, however, that it comes up against insurmountable obstacles. The law cannot, in fact, float above politics. It can be exercised only within a political community or result from the decision of several political units to ally themselves to one another in a way which suits them. That means that, as long as there is no world government, the right of humanitarian interference can only be a caricature of a right.

All justice needs a political power which serves it at least with executive force. In the absence of a world government, the power called to play the role of the planetary police can only be that of armed forces so strong that nobody can resist them. As the armies are always at the service of particular states, that therefore leads to sanctioning the hegemony of superpowers, of which it would be naïve to believe that they would not seek to serve their own interests first of all by covering their aggressions with a cloak of morality and justice. It follows from this that, among those presumed guilty, only the weak will be able to be punished while the powerful, who cannot be brought to punish themselves, will not be disturbed.[18] Now, a justice which is not the same for

---

17 *Jus ad bellum*, meaning 'right to wage war' in Latin, are the conditions under which it is considered acceptable under international law for a nation to declare war on another. *Jus in bello*, or 'laws of war', are the laws which apply in combat once a war is in progress, such as the Geneva Convention.-Ed.

18 Cf. Tzvetan Todorov, 'Les illusions d'une justice universelle', in *Le Monde des débats*, May 2001, p. 27. The most revealing is that, when the great powers judge that they, too, might one day need to submit to the general law, they abruptly retrace their steps. This is how the United States has constantly promoted the principle of human rights beyond its borders, even while contesting that the same standards might apply to them. They demanded the appearance of the Serbian President Milošević before the International Criminal Tribunal, even while making it known that, for their part, they do not recognise its jurisdiction. Cf. Stanko Cerovic, 'Le TPI, instrument de l'empire américain', in *Le Monde des débats*, May 2001, p. 26. As regards the right of humanitarian interference, David B. Rivkin, Jr. and Lee

all does not deserve this name. Recalling the saying of Proudhon,[19] '[W]hoever invokes humanity wants to cheat',[20] Carl Schmitt had already remarked that '[t]he concept of humanity is an especially useful ideological instrument of imperialist expansion, and in its ethical-humanitarian form it is a specific vehicle of economic imperialism'.[21] In any event, humanity is not a political concept. A 'world politics of human rights' is, therefore, equally a contradiction in terms.

The idea that in politics good can only engender good ignores what Max Weber[22] called the paradox of consequences. Historical experience shows that the best intentions can have catastrophic effects. It also shows that the right of interference never resolves any problem but tends, on the contrary, to multiply them, as one has been able to see in Kosovo, in Afghanistan or in Iraq. Democracy and freedoms are not imposed from outside, especially in one moment. Their establishment can only result from a local evolution, not from a forced conversion. Furthermore, the political authorities attacked or crushed as a result of the discussion of human rights do not disappear to the advantage of a pacified and more just world, but to the advantage of economic and financial institutions, which create social inequalities and tensions, exercised still more arbitrarily by multinational enterprises and financial markets. 'The ideology of human rights', affirms Alain Bertho, 'calls less for the liberation of peoples than for the police of the states'.[23] Hardly had the French Revolution proclaimed human rights

---

A. Casey wrote recently that it 'may prove to be one of the most potent weapons ever deployed against the United States', for 'has the potential to undermine American leadership in the post-Cold War global system' ('The Rocky Shoals of International Law', in *The National Interest*, New York, Winter 2000-2001, pp. 36-38). As an alternative, the authors express the wish that the United States 'actively work to shape international law in ways that both support [its] national interests and that are consistent with [its] philosophical foundations' (*ibid.*, p. 41).

19 Pierre-Joseph Proudhon (1809-1865) was a French politician and philosopher who opposed capitalism and did not believe in state ownership of property, instead believing that property should belong to workers' groups.-Ed.

20 *The Concept of the Political* (Chicago: University of Chicago Press, 2007), p. 54.-Ed.

21 *Ibid.*, p. 54.

22 Max Weber (1864-1920) was a German who is considered one of the founders of sociology. His principal work is *The Protestant Ethic and the Spirit of Capitalism.* Weber discusses the idea of the paradox of consequences in *Economy and Society.*-Ed.

23 *Contre l'Etat, la politique* (Paris: La Dispute, 1999), p. 104.

than, to render them more effective, it instituted the Terror.[24] From 1792 to 1801, it was in the name of 'freedom' that France was engaged in a politics of occupation, annexations and conquests. The right of humanitarian interference is equally belligerent. 'It is not excluded that, just as men make war "for a better peace"', wrote Julien Freund, 'it may happen that one day they may fight in the name of conceptions equally estimable concerning human rights'.[25] We are, quite precisely, there already. Bernard Kouchner[26] who, not so long ago, flattered himself that he 'found himself always on the side of those who receive the bombs and not of those who throw them', declares today, 'A preventive war is a notion which seems to me not only just, but which approximates to what, with others, we have proposed as a duty, and then a right, of interference'.[27] But the right of interference does not justify preventive war alone. By endowing the wars that it provokes with a moral character, by presenting them as 'just wars', it ends by criminalising the enemy, in making him a symbol of Evil: one who makes war in the name of humanity can only place his adversaries outside humanity. By definition, 'just war' is a total war.

∗

One knows that the doctrine of human rights, defining rights as attributes inherent in human nature, posits the individual as self-sufficient. 'The basic rights in the actual sense', emphasises Carl Schmitt,

---

24 The Reign of Terror was a period between 1793 and 1794 in France when the revolutionary National Convention, led by Robespierre, executed perceived enemies of the French Revolution, including not just members of the aristocracy, the priesthood and the old regime but even those who had supported the revolution but who held views in opposition to the Convention. Thousands of people were sentenced to death during this period.-Ed.

25 *Politique et impolitique* (Paris: Sirey, 1987), p. 198.

26 Bernard Kouchner (b. 1939) is a French socialist politician with a history of radical activism who served as French Foreign Minister from 2007 until 2010. In early 2003, when the U.S.-led war against Iraq was imminent, Kouchner declared himself to be in favour of removing Saddam Hussein from power, even though he believed that this should be accomplished by the United Nations and not by the United States acting unilaterally.-Ed.

27 *Le Monde*, 17 September 2002.

'are essentially rights of the free individual person'.[28] It is, besides, because human rights are the attributes of an isolated individual and of
a disengaged subject who is independent in relation to those like him,
for he is considered as one who finds in himself his essential *raisons
d'être*, rather than such reasons being posited as the antithesis of duties
that would be symmetrical to them. This individualism was originally
so marked that the Declaration of 1789 ignores the freedom of association, and more generally all forms of collective rights, its authors
condemning besides (the Le Chapelier Law, the Allarde decree)[29] all
the basically professional groupings. Collective rights are recognised
today, but human rights are still rights whose realisation is considered,
in the final analysis, to concern the individual alone, even when certain
of these rights can be realised only collectively.

'Modern humanism is an abstract subjectivism', writes Jean-Louis
Vullierme. 'It imagines men as preconstituted individuals, substances
that are universally bearers of the same attributes, apt to legitimate the
same demands in all circumstances according to formal rules deducible from a unique rationality'.[30] This individualism or atomism evidently implies contractualism: in the beginning, as soon as there are
only isolated individuals, one can explain the formation of societies
only by contract, a legal procedure characteristic of civil law: before
the market, only this can get round the great difficulty that there is
in founding the legitimacy of a society on the principle of the independence of the individual, that is to say, on 'the principle of the most

---

28 *Constitutional Theory* (Durham: Duke University Press, 2008), p. 203. The culture
    of rights, summarises Charles Taylor, is a triply individualist culture: '[I]t prizes
    autonomy; it gives an important place to self-exploration, in particular of feeling;
    and its visions of the good life generally involve personal commitment. As a
    consequence, in its political language, it formulates the immunities due people in
    terms of subjective rights. Because of its egalitarian bent, it conceives these rights
    as universal' (*Sources of the Self: The Making of the Modern Identity* [Cambridge:
    Cambridge University Press, 1989], pp. 305).

29 The Le Chapelier Law and the Allarde decree were passed by the revolutionary
    National Assembly in 1791, following the French Revolution. The laws banned
    guilds as well as forbade strikes and state intervention in the economy, proclaiming
    free enterprise to be the sole arbiter of French labour.-Ed.

30 'Questions de politique', in Michel Garcin (ed.), *Droit, nature, histoire: Michel
    Villey, philosophe du droit* (Aix-en-Provence: Presses universitaires d'Aix-Marseille,
    1985), p. 170.

asocial being that there is'.[31] However, in the doctrine of human rights, the social contract does not change the nature of the individuals. The society remains a simple sum of individual atoms with sovereign wills, all equally moved by the rational search for their best interest. Each agent defines his objectives by himself, in a voluntary manner, and adheres to society only on an instrumental basis. In other words, only the individual really exists, while society or the collectivity is only an abstraction, an illusion or a superimposed reality.

For theoreticians of rights, politics thus has nothing natural. In relation to the state of nature, it constitutes an artificial or imposed superstructure. This superstructure, in order to be legitimate, must be at the service of the individual and give up defining itself as an action taken by a collective being: 'The *aim* of every political association', one reads in Article 2 of the Declaration of 1789, 'is the conservation of the natural and inalienable rights of man'. At the core of society, man is thus not defined straightaway as a citizen, but first as a member of the 'civil society' (or private sphere), the latter itself being defined as the part of society which can rightly be subtracted from the political life (or public sphere). That is indeed why the theory of human rights gives priority to the *private* rights of individuals. As Marcel Gauchet writes, 'It is not a question of any version of human rights, but of a version defined exactly, which consists which involves exploiting the inherence of the rights in the individual against the associations of the citizen'.[32]

In the beginning, the theory of human rights seemed to be raised only against a particular political form — in the case of despotism. But, in fact, its critique is deployed against *every* form of politics. The key idea is that of an opposition of principle, always latent, between the individual and the community or collectivity to which he belongs. The individual would always be threatened by what is outside his individual being, in such a way that it is only by affirming his prerogatives as an individual that he can guard against this threat. According to this view, neither the society, nor the family, nor the public powers, nor the social relations, nor even the culture are perceived as being able to constitute a protection as well. This is the origin of the necessity of guaranteeing to individual actions an inviolable and 'sacred' sphere.

---

31 Pierre Manent, *Naissance de la politique modern* (Paris: Payot, 1977), p. 11.

32 *La religion dans la démocratie: Parcours de la laïcité* (Paris: Gallimard, 1998), p. 81.

It is thus not no exaggeration to say that the proclamation of these rights assumes, from the start, an anti-political sense. As Carl Schmitt remarks, it signifies that 'the liberty sphere of the individual is *unlimited* in principle, while the powers of the state are *limited* in principle.'[33] Concomitantly, the theory of human rights creates a radical novelty: a freedom independent of all participation in political affairs, a freedom of the individual separated from the freedom of the political community to which he belongs, an idea which in Antiquity would have been considered 'absurd, immoral and unworthy of a free man.'[34] (Carl Schmitt). Finally, if rights are unlimited in principle, the duties themselves can only be limited — both because, being linked to social life, they cannot be the opposite of rights inherent in human nature, and because it would be contradictory, from the point of view of the theory of rights, to imagine unlimited duties towards entities conceived as potentially menacing for the individual. In this perspective, certain questions are deliberately left aside, for example the question of knowing if and in what circumstances a collectivity can have rights in relation to the individuals that constitute it. In the best case, every restriction of rights by a political power can only possess the status of an exception.

A good illustration of the way in which the affirmation of the sovereignty of the individual necessarily antagonises the political organisation of a society is furnished by the way in which the French Revolution tried to reconcile human rights and those of the citizen — a question which, in many respects, resembles the old problem of the union of the soul and the body.Article 2 of the Declaration of 1791 affirms that the rights of the citizen have as their exclusive aim the conservation of human rights. This affirmation is repeated in Article 1 of the Declaration of 1793. Thereby, the Revolutionary right aims, quite evidently, to reconcile the subjective right and the objective right, the natural right and the positive right, to ensure the union of citizenship and one's membership in humanity. However, during the Revolution, 'natural' man is not really comprehensible except under the genre of citizen. One of the reasons for this is probably that the Revolutionary power succeeded an already existing state power, while the American declarations of rights aimed, in a totally different context, at fabricating

---

33 *Theory of the Constitution*, p. 197-198.

34 *Ibid.*, p. 198.-Ed.

a new political entity.[35] Rousseau, for his part, had already declared that he was for the primacy of the citizen in a famous page: 'We must therefore choose whether we will make a man or a citizen; we cannot do both.'[36] The authors of the Revolutionary texts themselves adhere to a civic-oriented conception of rights which goes together with a strong legalism, and this tendency is further reinforced by their desire to define the rights of the nation as a priority. In effect, the consecration of the sovereignty of the nation rapidly dominated that of the universal rights of the individual. 'The nation', writes Mona Ozouf, 'is not thought of as constituted of free and equal individuals, but endowed, from the very first days of the Revolution, with an absolute priority.'[37] The definition of man as a natural subject who needs to become the object of a positive legislation in order to be recognised as a subject of the law has thus sanctioned the primacy of the rights of the citizen — which permitted the Revolutionary power to legitimate the political recruitment of individuals.

Examining the definition of human rights and the rights of the citizen in the Declaration of 1789 from the theoretical angle, Karl Marx remarks for his part that, in liberal and bourgeois law, the joint development of these two spheres is rhetorically possible, but practically contradictory, insofar as it cuts man into two and assigns to him, within each sphere, aims that cannot be reconciled or even united.

Just as he sees very well that behind the right to work there is first the power of capital, Marx also sees that with the abstract generalisation of 'man', whose rights are proclaimed, the play of private interests is above all affirmed. That is why he denounces the formalism of human rights and their manipulation to the advantage of the propertied class which is alone capable of determining, by its laws, within what limits

35 Cf. Marcel Gauchet, *La révolution des droits de l'homme* (Paris: Gallimard, 1988); and Stéphane Rials (ed.), *La Déclaration des droits de l'homme et du citoyen* (Paris: Hachette, 1989).

36 *Jean Jacques Rousseau: His Educational Theories Selected from Émile, Julie and Other Writings* (Hauppauge: Barron's Educational Series, 1964), p. 9.

37 Preface to Ladan Boroumand, *La guerre des principes: Les assemblées révolutionnaires face aux droits de l'homme et à la souveraineté de la nation, mai 1789-juillet 1794* (Paris: Éditions de l'École des hautes études en sciences sociales, 1999), p. 8. Cf. also Elisabeth Guibert-Sledziewski, 'L'invention de l'individu dans le droit révolutionnaire', in *La Révolution et l'ordre juridique privé: Rationalité ou scandale? Actes du colloque d'Orléans* (Paris: CNRS-Université d'Orléans and PUF, 1988), pp. 141-149.

the freedom of every person should be exercised. The rights are considered as being valid for all, but in fact they are essentially reserved for the bourgeoisie. 'Thus none of the so-called rights of men', writes Marx, 'goes beyond the egoistic man, the man withdrawn into himself, his private interest and his private choice, and separated from the community as a member of civil society.'[38] To affirm that the end of all political association is the conservation of human rights, to make the rights of the citizen a 'simple means of conserving these professed human rights' comes down from that moment to placing the citizen at the service of the selfish man: '[M]an as bourgeois rather than man as citizen is considered to be the *proper* and *authentic* man... Actual man is recognized only in the form of an *egoistic* individual, *authentic* man, only in the form of *abstract citizen*.'[39] Marx's thesis has been explicitly criticised by Claude Lefort, who affirms that it is, on the contrary, the abstraction of human rights, their ahistorical and formal character, that constitutes their value and guarantees the possibility of having recourse to them in no matter what situation. It is precisely, says Lefort, because human rights are those of a man without determination that they can correspond to their definition: 'Human rights lead the law to a foundation which, in spite of its denomination, is shapeless, exists as it were within itself, and in this, eludes every power which intends to seize it.'[40] But Lefort does not explain how such rights, which no 'power' can seize, could be guaranteed and applied outside a political order, itself implying a power. This poses the more general problem of the implementation of the rights. Human rights derive in effect from the modern natural right, not from positive right. Now, as opposed to the latter, natural right does not by itself have at its disposal any means of restraint. It is a 'disarmed' right, and the modern natural right is

---

38 'On the Jewish Question', in *Writings of the Young Marx on Philosophy and Society* (Indianapolis: Hackett Publishing, 1997), pp. 236-237. From 'On the Jewish Question' (1843) to the writings of his maturity, Marx will never return to this judgment. Thereafter he will denounce not only human rights as formal rights, but also as rights in general, letting it be understood in this way that it is not in terms of right that one should think of politics. Cf. Bertrand Binoche, *Critiques des droits de l'homme* (Paris: PUF, 1989), pp. 97-112; and Georg Lohmann, 'La critica fatale di Marx ai diritti umani', in *Studi Perugini*, January-June 1998, pp. 187-199.

39 *Ibid.*, pp. 237, 240.

40 'Droits de l'homme et politique', in *L'invention démocratique* (Paris: Fayard, 1981), p. 66.

still more so than the ancient one to the extent that it does not recognise the social nature of man. Rights conceived as inalienable attributes of the subject, that is to say, rights that every man is justified in demanding that they be respected for the sole reason that he is a man, do not possess 'by themselves and in themselves either legal importance or significance' (Simone Goyard-Fabre). In order that they may acquire it, they should be sanctioned by rules of positive law, which can be conceived only within a society. Only positive law can say, in fact, whom such rights should benefit, who is harmed by a failure to apply them and in what, etc. In other words, subjective rights, posed as external to all social fact, can acquire an effective consistency only in a social context. That is an initial paradox. Régis Debray summarises it in these terms: 'One who wishes to be a mere individual to enjoy a fullness of freedom forgets that there are no human rights without the legal form of the state'.[41]

A second paradox results from the difficulty that there is in claiming that human rights can predominate over positive right in such a way that every political power should begin by recognising them, even while admitting that the practical validity of these rights depends on the capacity of this same political power to apply them. Bentham had already stigmatised this contradiction of contractualism, which consists in basing the rights of the citizen on human rights when the latter can have an effective existence only from the former. 'On the one hand', observes Julien Freund, 'one demands the respect of these rights for the same reason that one respects the dispositions of positive law, but, on the other, makes it known, with more or less perspicacity, that the validity of these rights should not depend on ordinary legislative examples since they aim at universality'.[42]Still more generally, that poses the question of the relations between politics and the law. The ideology of human rights, we have seen, posits the anteriority of natural law in relation to society and draws the argument from that to limit the prerogatives of politics. Now the law, being impotent by itself, always supposes something outside of itself to exercise itself. As

---

41 *L'Etat séducteur: Les révolutions médiologiques au pouvoir* (Paris: Gallimard, 1993), p. 161.

42 *Op. cit.*, p. 191. Freund concludes from this that one cannot even say of a declaration of human rights that it belongs to natural right inasmuch as even these rights can be effective only from the moment when they have been proclaimed: 'We are in the presence of a right whose nature remains indeterminable' (*ibid.*, p. 192).

Marcel Gauchet writes, 'the point of view of the law does not allow one to take account of the context in which the law may rule. It is here that one should pass to the political point of view. It is demanded by the extent of the limits to the ideas of a foundation in law'.[43]

The tension between human rights and those of the citizen, that is to say of man considered as a member of a particular political community, appears again in the discussions that have surrounded the arrival of 'the rights of the second generation', that is to say of collective or social rights.

These rights of the second generation (right to work, right to education, right to medical care, etc.) are of a completely different nature than individual rights. Sometimes qualified as 'equality rights' compared to 'freedom rights', as 'rights to' compared to 'rights of', or again of 'rights of recipience' compared to 'rights of action',[44] they represent, above all, beliefs permitting members of a society to demand or obtain positive services from the state. These are not so much natural *attributes* as *attributions* that a particular society which has reached a certain moment in its history thinks to be able to and be obliged to give its members. Not only do they 'presuppose an organised civil society which will be the guarantee of their efficacy'[45] but to the extent that they even support themselves on the notion of solidarity, they imply the social phenomenon and cannot be deduced from the pre-political nature of the individual. Finally, contrary to the rights of the first generation, which are unlimited in principle (one cannot restrain them without harming what they are based on), they are, on the contrary, limited, for every belief *vis-à-vis* others is limited by the executive capacities and the means of the others.

While the theory of individual rights tends to limit the power and the authority of the state, the institution of collective rights makes of the latter the privileged instrument of their implementation. The state is no longer expected to abstain, restrain itself or disengage itself, but, on the contrary, to implicate itself, to become engaged, indeed to establish itself as the exclusive provider of an ever-increasing number

---

43 'Les tâches de la philosophie politique', in *La Revue du MAUSS*, first quarter 2002, p. 292.

44 D. D. Raphael, *Problems of Political Philosophy* (London: Macmillan, 1970).

45 Jean-François Kervégan, 'Démocratie et droits de l'homme', in Gérard Duprat (ed.), *L'ignorance du peuple: Essai sur la démocratie* (Paris: PUF, 1998), p. 48.

of services. 'The recognition of social rights having the character of "beliefs"', writes Jean-François Kervégan, 'implies that sufficient power over the members of the city shall be conferred and recognised for it to be able to guarantee them the enjoyment of these rights, in spite of the possible opposition of particular interests among them and of some of these with regard to measures capable of harming them'.[46]

Such indeed is the reason for the hostility of liberal milieus to collective rights, which they qualify in the best of cases as 'fine ideals',[47] that is to say as pious wishes without real justification. If certain of these rights are reducible to individual cases, others, in fact, cannot be distributed: they have as debtors not individuals but collectivities. The right to speak one's language, for example, is inseparable from the right to the existence of the group which uses this language, and this second right conditions the first. Now, liberal individualism rejects the very idea that a collectivity can imagine itself attributing individual traits, in the case of rights, and postulates that the value of a possession depends on its conformity with the principle of the respect that one owes to the individual alone. That is why Hayek[48] violently denounces social rights, insofar as they derive from a distributive justice: '[A]ny policy aiming directly at a substantive ideal of distributive justice must lead to the destruction of the Rule of Law'.[49]

It would therefore be useless to deny, as Claude Lefort does,[50] the depth of the 'generation gap' separating individual rights from collective rights. Between the one and the other there is a difference of kind, not a difference of degree. This difference of kind goes well beyond the classical antinomy between equality, assimilated to justice, and freedom.[51] On the one hand, individual rights can cause an obstruction

---

46   *Ibid.*

47   'Lofty ideals', as Maurice Cranston writes, in *Human Rights Today* (London: Ampersand, 1962).

48   Friedrich Hayek (1899-1992) was an economist who was crucial to the development of the Austrian school of economics. He opposed collectivism and state control of the economy in favour of classical liberalism, holding that only the free market and limited government were the only effective method of organising societies.-Ed.

49   *The Road to Serfdom: Texts and Documents* (New York: Routledge, 2007), p. 117.

50   *Essais sur le politique* (Paris: Seuil, 1986).

51   'The more justice there is, the less freedom there is', writes Max Horkheimer. 'If one wishes to move towards equity, one should prohibit many things to men... But

to the realisation of collective rights, unless the reverse is true (that is why liberals and socialists mutually accuse each other of violating the former in the name of the latter, or the latter in the name of the former). On the other hand, a number of public or social goods are not divisible, which means that they have a significance only in a holistic understanding of social action. The institution of collective rights implies the recognition of the importance of the notion of belonging, and leads to the division of the subjects of right into groups, which is what the classical theory of human rights has always refused to do. The liberals draw an argument from these with which to criticise social rights. One could rightly draw the opposite conclusion from it: social rights, from the sole fact that they are social, are more credible than those drawn from an abstract individual 'nature', especially when they allow one to restore the notion of distributive justice to honour.

*

In public opinion, the fight for human rights is frequently presented as an aspect of the fight for democracy. 'The complete democratisation of Europe', declared Javier Pérez de Cuéllar in 1990, then Secretary-General of the United Nations, 'will be a reaffirmation of the universal character of the Declaration of Human Rights'. The same opinion has been expressed since then by Francis Fukuyama and by many other authors. In this perspective, democracy and human rights are considered to progress in tandem. The two expressions cannot contradict each other. They even become almost synonyms.

Regardless, this opinion has not been any less contested on several occasions. Examining the relation between democracy and human rights, Julien Freund said that it 'is not evident'. Their equation, writes Jean-François Kervégan, is at least 'problematic'.[52] Myriam Revault d'Allones adds that it 'does not go without saying'.[53] There are several reasons for this.

---

the more freedom there is, the more one who deploys its powers with superior skill than others will finally be capable of dominating them, and thus there will be less justice' (*Théorie critique* [Paris: Payot, 1978], p. 358).

52 *Art. cit.*, p. 42.

53 *Le dépérissement de la politique: Généalogie d'un lieu commun* (Paris: Flammarion-Champs, 2002), p. 284.

A primary reason is that democracy is a political doctrine, while human rights is a legal and moral doctrine, and that these two types of doctrines do not accord with each other spontaneously. As a political regime, democracy tends quite naturally to restrain that which is not democratic, and, more generally, that which is not political. The theory of human rights, on the contrary, tends to restrain the prerogatives of politics. But above all, as one has seen with regard to human rights and the rights of the citizen, the one and the other do not have the same subject. The ideology of human rights can only recognise abstract individuals, while democracy knows only citizens. Now, even if they use the same legal rhetoric, the rights of the citizen (equality before the law, freedom of petition, equal right of suffrage and vote, equal access to public jobs according to capacity, etc.) are fundamentally different from human rights. They are not attributes of man as man, but *capacities* related, not only to a particular political regime (democracy), but also, and especially, to a specific membership (a given political community). The theory of human rights gives the right to vote indiscriminately to all men insofar as they are men ('one man, one vote'). Democracy gives the right to vote to all the citizens but refuses it to non-citizens. 'The democratic rights of state citizenship', writes Carl Schmitt, 'presuppose the state citizen, the citoyen, living in the state, not individual free persons in the extra-state condition of "freedom". This means these democratic rights have an essentially political character'.[54]

A democratic regime, on the other hand, draws its legitimacy from the consent of the people, the latter being generally expressed by votes. In the final analysis, democracy is the regime which sanctions the sovereignty of the people. On the contrary, the discourse concerning human rights is given straightaway as a moral certainty, as a universal truth, considered to impose itself everywhere by the fact of its universality alone. Its value does not thus depend on a democratic ratification. Better still, it can oppose it.

'The problem of human rights', observes Revault d'Allonnes, 'arises from an individual foundation — the problem of the natural rights of the individual — which inevitably enters into conflict with the requisites of sovereignty'.[55] This tension can assume two aspects. On the one

54 *Constitutional Theory*, p. 207.

55 *Op. cit.*, p. 284.

hand, to the extent to which international law inspired by the theory of human rights — the right of interference — implies a limitation of the sovereignty of the state and of peoples, it also implies, in the heart of every democratic state, a limitation of popular sovereignty. On the other hand, the conditions under which the theory of human rights has been enunciated result in the suffrage itself no longer being recognised as sovereign except insofar as it does not contradict the postulates of this theory. From the perspective of human rights, explains Guy Haarscher, 'the democratic principle can be valid only within strict limits, which are precisely those of the philosophy of human rights: supposing that a single individual defends these latter against a majority opinion determined to violate them, it is this single person who, from the point of view of the contractualistic philosophy, [will have] adopted the sole legitimate attitude'.[56]

Since democratic votes do not go in the direction of human rights, they are therefore immediately rejected as 'irrational' and illegitimate. The same ideology is opposed to the people being consulted, for example by way of a referendum, on subjects considered as too 'sensitive'. A certain denunciation of 'populism' enters quite evidently into this context: when one broaches the question of 'human rights', the people are too often suspected of thinking badly.

'The recognition and the proclamation of human rights', further writes Jean-François Kervégan, 'implies that insurmountable limits are posed to sovereignty, whether it be monarchical or popular'.[57] Now, every limitation of popular sovereignty represents an attack against the very foundation of democracy. It is equivalent to an obligation made to the citizens to give up being governed by anyone except the leaders whom they have elected. It implies that the ultimate authority to which the citizens owe obedience is no longer that of their elected leaders, but that of international authorities or jurisdictions whose members, speaking, as it were, in the name of a revealed truth, do not have the least democratic legitimacy. Once the popular sovereignty is

---

56 *Philosophie des droits de l'homme* (Brussels: Éditions de l'Université de Bruxelles, 1987), p. 15.

57 *Art. cit.*, p. 43.

placed under certain conditions, it is a clear return to political and social heteronomy.[58]

It is significant that today, one reproaches authoritarian governments much less for lacking democratic principles than for not 'respecting human rights'. To palliate the political instability that hinders the planetary expansion of the markets, the Trilateral Commission,[59] established in 1973, and whose two principal theoreticians were Samuel Huntington[60] and Zbigniew Brzezinski,[61] had already expressed the wish to restrain the field of democratic practices in the countries of the Third World. 'To reply to these two demands — restrained democracy and the survival of capitalism', writes Edmond Jouve, 'an ingredient has been found: the ideology of human rights'.[62]

The redefinition of democracy as the 'regime that respects human rights' — that is to say, finally, its reduction to liberal democracy, is thus intellectually untenable.[63] but it is politically very profitable since

---

58 Cf. Robert Bork, 'The Limits of "International Law"', in *The National Interest*, Winter 1989-1990, p. 10. ('There can be no authentic rule of law among nations until nations have a common political morality or are under a common sovereignty. A glance at the real world suggests we have a while to wait.'-Ed.)

59 The Trilateral Commission is a think tank founded by David Rockefeller to facilitate economic cooperation between the United States, western Europe and Japan, although the list of nations which participate in it has grown since then. In 1975, the Commission issued a report entitled *The Crisis of Democracy*, which controversially criticised the 1960s as a period of an 'excess of democracy'.-Ed.

60 Samuel Huntington (1927-2008) was an American political scientist who became infamous for serving as an advisor to authoritarian regimes, such as South Africa in the 1980s. He famously postulated that nations in the process of transitioning into modernity must be cautious about not introducing democracy too quickly into their societies, and that repressive measures can actually be necessary and beneficial in the short term. More recently, he became well-known for his book *The Clash of Civilizations*, in which he theorized that the changing world order following the collapse of Communism would be defined by conflicts between cultural blocs, such as the West and the Islamic world.-Ed.

61 Zbigniew Brzeziński (b. 1928) was the National Security Advisor to the Carter administration from 1977 to 1981. Since then he has gained a reputation as a highly respected political analyst. In the past he has advocated an active role by economically advanced nations to counter instability brought about by economic inequalities in the Third World.-Ed.

62 *Le droit des peuples* (Paris: PUF, 1986), p. 52.

63 On the compatibility of the doctrinal foundations of liberalism and democracy, cf. Carl Schmitt, *Constitutional Theory, op. cit.* 'Democracy and liberalism are incompatible', writes Paul Piccone; 'liberal values are legitimate only if they are not

it allows one to reject as contradictory every democratic decision going against the ideology of human rights. Jean-Fabien Spitz affirms, however, that such a method is itself contradictory, for 'to say that the rights of individuals depend on reason and on nature, but to wish to protect them from discussion by all beings endowed with reason is to destroy their rational foundation'.[64] (Only a majority vote that would end in the abolition of democracy can be declared anti-democratic, for such a decision would contradict the end for which the vote is only a means.)

'One cannot strictly say anything about a politics of human rights', wrote Claude Lefort, 'so long as one has not examined if these rights have a really political significance'. Already in 1980, in a historical article, Marcel Gauchet had precisely affirmed that 'human rights are not politics'.[65] On these terms, he defined therein 'the greatest danger that the return to human rights hides: falling into the rut and the impasse of an idea of the individual against society, succumbing to the old illusion that one can base oneself on the individual and start from the individual, from his demands and his rights, to return to society. As if one could disjoin the search for an individual autonomy from the effort towards a social autonomy'.[66] 'Human rights', he concluded, 'are not politics insofar as they do not expose us to the entirety of the society in which they are introduced. They can become politics only on the condition that one is able to recognise and one gives oneself the means to surmount the alienating dynamism of the individualism that they diffuse as their natural counterpart'.[67]

Twenty years later, Gauchet published a new article in which he resumes and deepens the same subject.[68] He does not limit himself to reaffirming that the 'politics of human rights' leads to collective impo-

---

imposed from above by a central government pretending to know better' ('Ten Counter-Theses on the New Class Ideology: Yet Another Reply to Rick Johnstone', in *Telos* 119, Spring 2001, p. 153).

64 'Républicanisme et droits de l'homme', in *Le Débat*, November-December 1997, p. 65.

65 'Les droits de l'homme ne sont pas une politique', in *Le Débat*, Paris, July/August 1980. The text was republished in *La démocratie contre elle-même*, pp. 1-26.

66 *Ibid.*, pp. 17-18.

67 *Ibid.*, p. 26.

68 'Quand les droits de l'homme deviennent une politique', in *Le Débat*, May/August 2000. The text was republished in *La démocratie contre elle-même*, pp. 326-385.

tence. He shows there also that, in wishing to assume such a politics, democracy undermines 'the foundations on which it rests and the instruments that it needs'.

The ideology of human rights, he explains, isolates the legal element in societies to the detriment of politics and social history: 'We are witnesses to a revenge of rights and, concomitantly, of an eclipse of politics and of social history'.[69] This ideology argues, besides, in the name of strictly *individual* rights. Now, 'if there is a danger on the horizon, it is that of the weakening of the collective before the affirmation of individuals'.[70] Every democratic politics must, in effect, recognise that the society which it governs exceeds the simple sum of its constituent individuals, for fault of which there could not be a general will. That is why 'the politics of human rights as a democratic politics runs aground on the foundation. It runs aground in that it contributes to produce a society whose global design eludes its members. It can, indeed, enlarge the prerogatives of the individual in society; the more it succeeds in that, the more the figure of the whole weakens in its coherence, the less it is intelligible and governable... The politics of human rights turns its back and can only turn its back on the perspectives of an authentic government of the collective by itself'.[71]

Now, as Gauchet clarifies further elsewhere, democracy 'is and should be the government of the collectivity by itself in its whole, and not only in its parts. It is and should be self-government of the political community as such, without which the prerogatives of right of the members and the constituents of this community are finally revealed to be illusory. The democracy of rights is a truncated democracy which loses sight of the properly political dimension of democracy; it forgets the fact of the political community, a fact at the level of which is determined, in the final analysis, the existence of democracy... The installation of the individual subject of right in the plenitude of his prerogatives brings about the obscuring of the collective political subject of democracy'.[72]

'There are two principal ways of conceiving of a metapolitical humanity, a humanity having surmounted or surpassed its political

69 *Ibid.*, p. 335.

70 *Ibid.*, p. 378.

71 *Ibid.*, p. 381.

72 'Les tâches de la philosophie politique', *art. cit.*

condition', notes Pierre Manent. 'This can be a humanity organised according to the law, or this can be a humanity living according to its morality'.[73] The ideology of rights unites the one and the other, and that is why it can only *lack* politics. But it lacks it also, and especially, because it has as its subject an abstract man, posited as in the 'state of nature', that is to say, in the pre-social state. Hannah Arendt had already noticed it: 'Because philosophy and theology are always concerned with *man*, because all their pronouncements would be correct even if there were only one or two men or only identical men, they have found no valid philosophical answer to the question: what is politics?'[74]

The notion of the individual on which the entire discourse of human rights is based is, in fact, a remarkably impoverished notion, since the only thing that qualifies an individual is that he is an individual. (One can even ask oneself, in these conditions, if it is reasonable to attribute anything at all to him.) According to the doctrine of rights, it is by positing man as an individual that one reaches his essence. In reality, a man deprived of all his concrete characteristics is not at all a 'man in himself'. He is no longer anything, for he has undergone the 'loss of all human relationship'.[75] 'The mistake of human rights with regard to historical and political reality', writes Myriam Revault d'Allonnes, 'reveals, above all, the impasses of a naturalistic conception that is inevitably turned into its opposite. Testing it against the facts — that is to say, against the loss of *political* qualities considered substantial — what is discovered is not the permanent substratum of a human nature, it is a pure indetermination deprived of meaning'.[76]

The first theoreticians of human rights were not wrong to refer to human nature. But it is the notion that they formed of it that was inconsistent. One knows today — one has known it for a long time — that man is a social being, that the existence of men did not precede their coexistence; in short, that society is the perspective in which, from its origins, the human presence in the world has been recorded. Just as there is no spirit that is not incarnated, there is no individual that is not situated in a determined socio-historical context. Membership

---

73 *Art. cit.*, p. 501.

74 *The Promise of Politics* (New York: Schocken Books, 2005).

75 Hannah Arendt, *The Origins of Totalitarianism*, p. 297.

76 *Op. cit.*, p. 283.

in humanity is thus never immediate, but mediated: one belongs to it only through the intermediary of a particular collectivity or a given culture. It is impossible for man to define himself simply as an individual because he necessarily lives in a community, where he is connected to values, norms, shared meanings, and because the totality of these relations, these practices — in a word, everything that constitutes his living environment and surrounds his being, is not superimposed but, on the contrary, *constitutive* of his self.Man needs a community to live and to live well. But 'the famous saying of Aristotle, that man is a political animal, does not mean only that man is naturally made to live in society; it also means that man naturally asks to lead a political life, and to participate actively in the life of the political community'.[77] 'We call those acts just', writes Aristotle, 'that tend to produce and preserve happiness and its components for the political society'.[78]

Now, it is simply impossible to think and to organise a political body strictly in terms of individualism. 'A *society* therefore can no more be decomposed into *individuals*, than a geometric surface can be resolved into lines, or a line into points', said Auguste Comte.[79] 'An individual is an isolated knot', wrote Raimundo Panikkar more recently, 'a person is the entire fabric that is outside this knot, a fragment of the total fabric that constitutes the real... It is undeniable that, without the knots, the fabric would come undone; but without the fabric, the knots would not even exist'.[80] He deduces from this that every political plan implies a certain form of holism. In holism, society is anterior to the individual, as 'the whole is necessarily prior to the part'.[81] But the parts encompassed by the whole are not reducible o this whole, and it is in this that holism is distinguished from collectivism. The essential difference is that, in collectivism, the social entities are imposed absolutely on the individuals, whereas, in holism, it is the capacities of the

---

77 Jacques Maritain, *Les droits de l'homme* (Paris: Desclée de Brouwer, 1989), p. 84.

78 Aristotle, *Nicomachean Ethics*, Book 5, Chapter 1, in *A New Aristotle Reader* (Princeton: Princeton University Press, 1987), p. 408.

79 Auguste Comte (1798-1857) was a prominent French Positivist philosopher. This quotation is from his *System of Positive Polity*, vol. 2 (New York: Lenox Hill, 1968), p. 153.

80 'La notion de droits de l'homme est-elle un concept occidental?', in *Diogène*, October-December 1982, p. 100.

81 Aristotle, *Politics* (New York: Hackett Publishing, 1998), Book 1, Chapter 2, p. 4.-Ed.

individuals that depend on their social relations. This dependence is therefore not of a causal nature, but constitutive and reciprocal. From this perspective, the common good is neither the good proper to the whole nor the simple sum of particular goods; it is a good common to the parts and to the whole.

It is evident from this, if one admits that the defence and promotion of rights require as a priority the affirmation of politics, that, in attacking politics, in seeking unceasingly to reduce its prerogatives, the theory of rights undermines the very foundations of its implementation. A man can have rights only in a political context, in a political mode of life shared in common, because every right depends on the socio-historical conditions in which it is affirmed.[82] Just as formal rights are rights without weight (the right to work is not enough to find a job, and the right to education does not mean very much when the public powers do not have the financial means to ensure free instruction), the individual in himself cannot be a true subject of right. The rights can only be predicates of citizenship. 'If man attains humanity by becoming a citizen', observes Myriam Revault d'Allonnes, 'that is to say, by acquiring a political status and if, reciprocally, he loses his properly human qualities in losing this same status, human rights imply an exercise that is rooted in citizenship'.[83] Men, inversely, can acquire rights only in the midst of a specific polity, in a life context that concretely guarantees the power of benefiting from it. Which comes back to saying that, in the final analysis, the rights affirm and express the difference between men, never their identity.[84]

But one should go farther and question the very occasion of continuing to speak using the language of rights. As the theory of human rights is intrinsically associated with the liberal ideology, every attempt to give it a non-liberal reformulation is very likely to fail. It would be better to realise that the rights that one commonly invokes are not so much rights as *duties* of the governing, and, as a counterpart, *capacities* and *freedoms* that it is legitimate for the governed to demand if they are refused them.

---

82 Cf. Michael Walzer, *Spheres of Justice: A Defense of Pluralism and Equality* (New York: Basic Books, 1983), who shows that abstract egalitarianism does not allow one to think of justice for the simple reason that the question of justice can only be posed in relation to a determined community.

83 *Op. cit.*, p. 291.

84 Cf. Hannah Arendt, *On Revolution* (New York: Viking Press, 1963).

It is thus not a question, of course, of abandoning the defence of freedoms to the ideology of human rights, and much less of criticising the latter with a view to legitimising despotism. It is a question, on the contrary, of showing that the necessary fight against all forms of tyranny and oppression is a fundamentally political question which, as such, should be resolved politically. It is a question, in other words, of abandoning the legal sphere and the field of moral philosophy to affirm that the power of the political authority must be limited, not because the individuals enjoy, by nature, unlimited rights, but because a polity where despotism reigns is a bad political society; that the legitimacy of the resistance to oppression does not derive from an innate right, but from the necessity for the political authority to respect the freedom of the members of society; in short, that men should be free not because they 'have the right to that', but because a society where the fundamental freedoms are respected is *politically better* than — and, moreover, morally preferable to — a society where they are not.

That implies returning to citizenship conceived as an active participation in public life, and not as a notion which can be manipulated with a view to obtaining rights, the value of a principle. 'The acceptance of the minimal requirements of a democratic political order — the strict equality of rights and duties of each person', writes Jean-François Kervégan in this context, 'forces one to renounce all metaphysical, anthropological or even moral foundations of human rights, and especially of those that are fundamental, in favour of a strictly political foundation, that is to say, supported on the sole principle of the civic (and not natural, for nothing is less egalitarian than 'nature') equality of the citizen-individuals'.[85]

At the same time, that leads at the same time to rehabilitating the notion of *membership* in a political community, without which freedom, equality and justice are only inoperative abstractions. Far from enclosing the individual or threatening his being, this membership gives him, on the contrary, 'the possibility of being a significant individual', as Revault d'Allonnes writes, who adds, 'To found human rights "politically", one must think of politics and citizenship, not only in the secondary perspective of a guarantee of subjective natural rights, but also as the original condition which founds the effective exercise of the communal life. But — and the two things are evidently related — one

---

85 *Art. cit.*, p. 51.

must also review the question of the individualist foundation of society and think of individual uniqueness in terms of *uniqueness of membership* or even of *plural uniqueness*. The latter is not based on the ground of an individual foundation but on that of a relation to the common world. For, if the "right to have rights" is inseparable from membership in an organised political community — which, from this fact, cannot be reduced to an association of individuals — the irreplaceable uniqueness of a human being is not related to his self-sufficient foundation but to the memberships which make his individuation possible'.[86]

Finally, one must abandon the idea that there is necessarily a contradiction between individual freedom and social life, and simultaneously redefine freedom in a sense that is in accord with what Benjamin Constant[87] called 'the freedom of the Ancients',[88] and Isaiah Berlin 'positive freedom',[89] which is indissociable from an active participation in public life, whereas the freedom of the Moderns, or negative freedom, consists in a series of rights allowing one to protect oneself from this obligation.

Freedom is not only a personal power. It needs a social field to exercise itself. That is why one could not be satisfied with the definition figuring in Article 4 of the Declaration of Rights of 1789: 'Freedom consists in being able to do anything which does not harm others'. On the one hand, individual autonomy and the free expression of capacities and merits are not subjective rights but correspond, on the contrary, to an imperious political and social necessity. (Public education, for example, is not at all the result of some 'right to education' without which it would be free, but optional. What makes it obligatory is the recognition that instruction constitutes a social good.) On the other hand, individual freedom is never accomplished in a society that is

---

86 *Op. cit.*, pp. 294-295.

87 Benjamin Constant (1767-1830) was a Swiss-born French aristocrat and philosopher who is regarded as one of the first liberal theorists, viewing the Britain of his day as a model state which combined a monarchy with a democratic order driven by the free market. He opposed the French Revolution for its despotic tendencies.-Ed.

88 Constant outlines this idea in 'The Liberty of the Ancients Compared with That of the Moderns', in *Political Writings* (Cambridge: Cambridge University Press, 1988).-Ed.

89 Berlin first discussed this concept in his book *Liberty* (Oxford: Oxford University Press, 2002).-Ed.

not free, which comes back to saying that there is no private freedom without public freedom. 'The aim of the ancients was the sharing of social power among the citizens of the same fatherland', writes Benjamin Constant.[90] That means that freedom is also, first, a political problem — and not a problem of 'rights'. Such a freedom precedes and conditions justice, instead of being a result of it.

Let us add that one of the best means of defending freedoms consists in having recourse to the principle of subsidiarity,[91] which delegates to the superior authority only those tasks that cannot be accomplished at the lower levels or the local level, thus permitting one to return to a more rigorous conception of right: to establish (or re-establish) right is not to attribute authority to individuals the 'right' to obtain something, but to *give* them what is due to them, or to *return* to them, individually and collectively, in a concrete manner, that which has been unjustly taken away from them by a third party or by the state.

*

The historians often see in the English Magna Carta of 15 June 1215[92] the first text that 'constitutionally' enunciated human rights. This interpretation is anachronistic. Just like the Spanish Magna Carta of King Alphonso de Leon[93] which had preceded it in 1188, the Magna Carta is a document that is limited to politically establishing political freedoms. Carl Schmitt emphasises that it is 'considered historically, is only one of many examples of medieval agreements between prince

---

90 *Political Writings* (Cambridge: Cambridge University Press), p. 317.

91 Subsidiarity is a principle which emphasises the importance of the people having as much decision-making power as possible in regard to the issues which affect them, while decisions regarding the welfare of the larger community are left to the central government.-Ed.

92 King John was forced to sign the Magna Carta into law by the feudal barons in order to limit the powers of the monarch and protect their own privileges. It guarantees specific rights to freemen under English law, and was a crucial step in the development of England into a constitutional monarchy. It remains in force to this day.-Ed.

93 Alfonso IX (1171-1230) was King of León and Galicia, in what is modern-day Spain. He convened the Cortes Generales, or General Court, which is credited with being the first representative parliament in Europe, and which has continued to the present day.-Ed.

and feudal lords'.[94] It is, in fact, a question, in the form of a royal concession, of a pact of public law which guarantees to the feudal aristocracy a certain number of freedoms and protects it against eventual abuses of royal power. It is the same with the Habeas Corpus Act of 1679 (a guarantee against arbitrary arrests)[95] and of the Bill of Rights of 1689,[96] about which Schmitt writes, 'They are, in fact, contractual or statutory regulations of the rights of English barons or citizens, which in the course of a gradual development certainly assumed the character of modern principles, but they do not correspond to the original meaning of basic rights.'[97]

Freedom, in any case, has been a European concept since its origin. Ancient Greece was the first to proclaim its benefits. But it is especially in the north of Europe that its value seems to have been celebrated most constantly. Tacitus,[98] already, said that he was surprised to learn that, among the Germans, the kings were elected and the power to designate them always belonged to assemblies. The Germans, he adds, do not know of obligatory tax and only know voluntary contributions. What the Roman historian says of the status of women shows equally to what degree the freedom of the person was recognised in the countries of the North since the most ancient times.

In France, where the monarchy ceased to be elective only after Louis IX,[99] this ideal of freedom was kept alive throughout the Middle

---

94 *Constitutional Theory*, p. 178.

95 The Habeas Corpus Act was passed by the English Parliament. Although *habeas corpus* rights had existed in England for centuries prior to the Act, it strengthened the citizens' protection from prosecution for wrongful arrest.-Ed.

96 The Bill of Rights, passed by the English Parliament, limited the powers of the monarch and strengthened the Parliament's ability to govern without interference, among other achievements, such as guaranteed freedom of speech, the right of the citizenry to bear arms, and the abrogation of Church courts in favour of civil courts.-Ed.

97 *Constitutional Theory*, p. 197.

98 Publius Cornelius Tacitus (56 CE?-117 CE?) was a Roman Senator and historian who wrote a number of works, including one of the earliest accounts of the Germanic tribes, *Germania*.-Ed.

99 Louis IX (1214-1270), also known as St. Louis, was a Crusader who was highly regarded by his people and was known for his devotion. For more on the transition from elective to hereditary monarchy, see Alain de Benoist's book, *The Problem of Democracy* (London: Arktos, 2011), pp. 15-16.-Ed.

Ages. Describing the feudal regime, Fustel de Coulanges[100] writes, 'At the top of the hierarchy, the king was surrounded by his great vassals. Each of these vassals was himself surrounded by his own feudatories and he could not pronounce the least judgment without them... The king could neither make a new law, nor modify the existing laws, nor raise a new tax without the consent of the country... If one looks at the institutions of this regime from close quarters, and if one observes their meaning and significance, one will see that they were all directed against despotism. However great the diversity that seems to reign in this regime, there is, however, one thing that unites them: this thing is obsession with absolute power. I do not think that any regime better succeeded than that in rendering arbitrary rule impossible... Feudalism was an association of free men'.[101]

The end of the feudal regime marked the beginning of the disintegration of this system under the influence of Roman authoritarianism and the deadly blows of the centralised state. Little by little, hereditary royalty implemented a juridical-administrative centralisation at the expense of intermediary bodies and regional assemblies. While the communal revolution sanctioned the power of the nascent bourgeoisie, the regional parliaments ceased to be equal assemblies and became meetings of royal officers. Having become absolute, the monarchy supported itself upon the bourgeoisie to liquidate the last resistances of the nobility.

But there were also some theoreticians, even in France, who denounced centralisation, juridical-administrative rationalisation and royal absolutism, the mere imitation of divine absolutism. This demand is sometimes made in the name of 'the fundamental laws of the kingdom', sometimes by invoking the ancient Celtic or Germanic freedoms.

---

100 Numa Denis Fustel de Coulanges (1830-1889) was a French historian who felt that the modern-day French state should more closely emulate the societies of ancient Greece, Rome and France.-Ed.

101 'Considérations sur la France' (1870-1871), cited in François Hartog, Le XIXe siècle et l'histoire: Le cas Fustel de Coulanges (Paris: Seuil-Points, 2001), pp. 307-309. Fustel refutes, in passing, the objection that one could make against him by citing serfdom: 'Serfdom, far from having been the essence of feudalism, was never even a feudal institution... Not only was it not the feudal regime that created servitude; it was, on the contrary, that which caused it to disappear in the long run' (ibid., p. 309).

The system of freedom was 'found in the woods', Montesquieu[102] would say, in order to recall the aristocratic and Germanic origin of the idea of freedom. The same argument was maintained from the end of the Seventeenth century by the entire 'Germanist' movement (Henry de Boulainvilliers, Le Laboureur, Louis Adrien Le Page),[103] who then strongly opposed the 'Romanist' movement (the Abbé Dubos, the Marquis d'Argentons, Jacob Nicolas Moreau).[104] Following the example of Althusius and the Monarchomachs,[105] great adversaries of the theories of Jean Bodin,[106] its partisans repeated incessantly that, in the past, the kings never had absolute power. Some, like Boulainvilliers,[107] defended the doctrine of popular sovereignty and the thesis of an original nation

---

102 Charles de Secondat, Baron de Montesquieu (1689-1755) was a French Enlightenment philosopher who is best-known for *The Spirit of the Laws*, which was a fundamental work in the development of modern democratic ideology. Montesquieu used this phrase, in *The Spirit of the Laws*, to describe the fact that England and France were linked by their mutual inheritance of the political beliefs of the ancient Germanic nations.-Ed.

103 The Germanists were a movement in Eighteenth-century France who held that the French aristocracy was descended from the Nordic Franks who had conquered France, and that the underclass of the Third Estate was descended from the native Gauls. In their view, only the aristocrats had the right to rule France, and the aristocracy actually constituted a separate, and superior, race in opposition to the Third Estate.-Ed.

104 The Romanists believed that the Franks had been invited into Gaul at the request of the native populace in order to rule, and that they had not conquered Gaul by force.-Ed.

105 The Monarchomachs were a group of writers in France in the late Sixteenth century who believed that monarchs should only govern through their magistrates and officers, who would govern according to the peoples' desires. The Monarchomachs saw the citizenry as a collective body and believed that it possessed an innate knowledge of what was good that was unknown to the monarch. Controversially, the Monarchomachs also said that monarchs who persecuted the Church could be killed on the grounds that he was violating the contract between God and the people.-Ed.

106 Jean Bodin (1530-1596) was a French jurist who established the divine right of monarchs to rule, based on his understanding of ancient Roman law.-Ed.

107 *An Historical Account of the Antient Parliaments of France*, 2 vols. (London: J. Brindley, 1739). On the debate around the ancient 'Germanic freedoms', in France as well as in Germany, cf. also Lucien Calvié, "'Liberté', "libertés" et "liberté(s) germaniques(s)": une question franco-allemande avant et après 1789', in *Mots* 16, 1988, pp. 9-33; and Jost Hermand and Michael Niedermeier, *Revolutio germanica: Die Sehnsucht nach der 'alten Freiheit' der Germanen, 1750-1820* (Bern-Frankfurt am Main: Peter Lang, 2002).

where property was shared. This doctrine would be repeated later by Augustin Thierry.[108]

Another particularly interesting movement is classical republicanism (or civic humanism),[109] whose essential principles have been recalled in the contemporary age by authors like John G. A. Pocock, Quentin Skinner and, more recently, Philip Pettit. This school of thought is principally related to the Roman Republican tradition (Sallust[110] and Livy)[111] and more distantly to Greece (Polybius[112] and Aristotle), but also to Machiavelli, to the Florentine and Venetian humanists, to the English Republicans, and thus to Montesquieu, Rousseau and Jefferson.[113]

In England, the neo-Roman theory of civil freedom appeared in the Seventeenth century. Its representatives, Henry Parker, John Milton, Algernon Sidney and, above all, James Harrington, reveal a strictly political conception of freedom, and defend the thesis of a parliamentary and popular sovereignty, which resulted in their being violently attacked by Thomas Hobbes. The notion of civil liberty is for them

---

108 Augustin Thierry (1795-1856) was a French historian. Like the earlier Germanists, he believed that the rise of parliamentary democracy was tied to the culture of the Nordic Normans who had conquered Britain. He also studied the Medieval Communes as precursors of the modern liberal state.-Ed.

109 Classical republicanism was an idea that originated in the Renaissance among scholars who studied the works of the ancient Greeks and Romans, viewing society as being based on the social contract. While it does not reject the role of a monarch in society, it does see the most important element of society to be the prevention of the rise of tyranny.-Ed.

110 Gaius Sallustius Crispus (86-35 BCE) was a Roman historian who favoured the people's assemblies, as opposed to the rule of the old Roman aristocracy as represented by the Senate.-Ed.

111 Titus Livius (59 BC-17 AD) was a Roman historian who wrote an enormous history of Rome.-Ed.

112 Polybius was an Arcadian historian of the Second century BCE, and author of *The Histories*. He lived in Rome and studied the form of government of the Republic. He developed the idea of separation of powers between the branches of government which were later influential upon Cicero, Montesquieu and the United States Constitution.-Ed.)

113 Cf. John G. A. Pocock, *The Machiavellian Moment* (Princeton: Princeton University Press, 1975); Philip Pettit, *Republicanism: A Theory of Freedom and Government* (Oxford: Clarendon Press, 1997); and Quentin Skinner, *Liberty before Liberalism* (Cambridge: Cambridge University Press, 1998). Cf. also Jean-Fabien Spitz, *La liberté politique: Essai de généalogie conceptuelle* (Paris: PUF, 1995).

tied to the classical ideal of the *civitas libera* or 'free state', reanimated in the Italian Renaissance by the defenders of republican *libertà*, in particular Machiavelli in his *Discourses on Livy* (1514-1519). When they speak of 'natural rights and freedoms', it is thus never with regard to the individual but to what Milton and Harrington call 'common liberty', 'free government' or 'commonwealth'. Celebrating the 'civic virtues', the Neo-Romans at the same time rehabilitate politics to the degree where public institutions can contribute to the exercise of these virtues (whose first cause resides, nevertheless, in the social customs, traditions and practices). Their principal thesis is that man can be truly free only in a free state. They therefore reject the thesis according to which coercive force is the only one that would threaten individual freedoms, and emphasise that living collectively in a state of dependence already constitutes a source and a form of constraint. 'A free state', writes Quentin Skinner, 'is a community in which the actions of the political body are determined by the will of the totality of its members'.[114] In such a state, the laws must be applied with the consent of all the members of the political body, which implies their active participation in public life at the same time as the rejection of absolute monarchy as tyranny.

From such a perspective, far from freedom being called upon to manifest itself in a privileged manner in a private sphere always threatened by political authority, being free means, first, to be able to take part in decisions whose locus is the social and political life, avoiding constraint and coercion, and thus contributing to the maintenance of collective freedoms. Freedom then becomes a form of social relationship: I cannot be free without the other members of my community being so equally. That means that there is only shared freedom, and that the rules to which the members of a political community conform constitute their common possession. The law, besides, ceases to be the enemy of freedom, for the intervention of the public powers can help in its realisation. The collectivity governs itself, not in terms of rights, but thanks to the participation of all.

'The first distinctive trait of a republican political philosophy', writes Jean-Fabien Spitz, 'is the affirmation according to which the rights that the citizens possess are not fixed by a philosophical reason that scrutinises nature, but by a common deliberation in which one tries to

---

114 *Op. cit.*, p. 25.

eliminate partialities by confronting them with nature and to attain norms that everybody may find legitimate... The rule is no longer, further, the expression of the cumulative interests of the greatest number, but of a shared conviction'.[115] The republic is thus composed 'of citizens who address not only the question of the institutional dispositions most favourable to the advancement of their own interests, but also the question of the norms of a legitimate and morally acceptable collective existence'.[116]

Jean-Fabien Spitz further clarifies, 'The republicans...refuse to conceive rights solely as instruments necessary for the accomplishment of a collection of essential duties, founded on nature and imposed from outside on every human will. On the contrary, they wish to conceive rights as the product of a democratic deliberation bearing on the kind of life we wish to lead collectively, and on the common principles around which the members of a republic wish to unite... The republicans thus consider that there is something profoundly erroneous in the idea of rights that are not social, anterior to all properly political deliberation: the rights are not qualities attached to the individuals outside all political society, but qualities which can only belong to citizens; these are not natural "trumps" with which the individuals could cut the decisions of the collectivities of which they are members, but principles of existence around which the societies are built'.[117]

The theory of civic republicanism which has been progressively dethroned in the Anglo-Saxon countries since the Eighteenth century by liberalism has sometimes approached the theses of the communitarian school, from which, however, it deviates on certain points (notably in Philip Pettit).

Extending in many respects the Hegelian critique of Kant, the communitarian critique of the ideology of rights is rooted in an essential conception of the good. The communitarians subordinate that which is right to the respect for a certain number of intrinsic goods, constitutive of the good life, a procedure antithetical to the liberal conception of rights. Affirming that the discussion of human rights ignores not only cultural diversity, but also the social basis of personal identity, they show that the rights belonging to a subject disconnected from

---

115 'Républicanisme et droits de l'homme', *art. cit.*, p. 51.

116 *Ibid.*

117 *Ibid.*, p. 52.

every communitarian relationship, or in any case, capable of revoking the commitments that result from it, are necessarily empty of meaning, since it is, on the contrary, the fact of belonging to a collectivity that constitutes the field of meaning from which it is possible to have rights: if there is no common social good, the rights accorded to the individuals are only an illusion.[118]

The majority of the communitarians nevertheless recognise individual rights, but contest the formulation which the liberals give to them. Among them, the critique of the liberal conception of rights generally takes two paths. The first consists in showing that, in according primacy to individual rights, liberalism neglects the communitarian dimension of human life which is indispensable to the constitution of the self as well as to the definition of a good life. The second resides in the affirmation that the justifications advanced to defend this prioritisation of individual rights rests on erroneous presuppositions concerning human nature. The communitarians also contest the autonomous character of the theory of rights, and affirm that it should at least be supported on a more general theory of moral action or of virtue, the latter having as its principal object to question oneself on what it is good to be, and not on what it is right to do.[119]If one refers to Ancient thought or to the Medieval tradition, to civic republicanism or to the theoretical works of the communitarian school, there is no shortage of sources, there is, in any case, no shortage of sources that allow us to found the necessary freedom without having recourse to liberal ideology, and to defend it in a more coherent and assured manner than the discussion of human rights does. It is beyond this

---

118 Cf. notably Alasdair MacIntyre, *After Virtue: A Study in Moral Theory* (Notre Dame: University of Notre Dame Press, 1981); Charles Taylor, *La liberté des modernes* (Paris: PUF, 1997) and *Sources of the Self: The Making of Modern Identity, op. cit.*; and Michael Sandel, *Liberalism and the Limits of Justice* (Cambridge: Cambridge University Press, 1982). For a more general critique of the 'discussion of rights', cf. also Richard E. Morgan, *Disabling America: The 'Rights Industry' in Our Time* (New York: Basic Books, 1984); Joseph Ratz, *The Morality of Freedom* (Oxford: Clarendon Press, 1986); and Mary Ann Glendon, *Rights Talk: The Impoverishment of Political Discourse* (New York: Free Press, 1991).

119 The right to property, for example, cannot be declared just in itself, independently of the good or bad uses made of it. Cf. Charles Taylor, 'Atomism', in A. Kontos (ed.), *Powers, Possessions and Freedom: Essays in Honour of C. B. Macpherson* (Toronto: University of Toronto Press, 1979).

discussion that, to repeat the fine formula of Pierre Chaunu,[120] 'the capacity to say *us* authentically, thus to resist the absolute *I*' is affirmed.

---

120 Pierre Chaunu (1923-2009) was a French historian who specialised in Latin American history. A Gaullist, Chaunu wrote several books describing the demographic self-destruction that is being committed by European nations as a result of their demographic decline, describing this phenomenon as the 'White plague'.-Ed.

Other books published by Arktos:

Revolution from Above
by Kerry Bolton

The Owls of Afrasiab
by Lars Holger Holm

The WASP Question
by Andrew Fraser

Why We Fight
by Guillaume Faye

De Naturae Natura
by Alexander Jacob

It Cannot Be Stormed
by Ernst von Salomon

The Saga of the Aryan Race
by Porus Homi Havewala

Against Democracy and Equality: The European New Right
by Tomislav Sunic

The Problem of Democracy
by Alain de Benoist

The Jedi in the Lotus
by Steven J. Rosen

Archeofuturism
by Guillaume Faye

A Handbook of Traditional Living

Tradition & Revolution
by Troy Southgate

Can Life Prevail?
A Revolutionary Approach to the Environmental Crisis
by Pentti Linkola

Metaphysics of War:
Battle, Victory & Death in the World of Tradition
by Julius Evola

The Path of Cinnabar: An Intellectual Autobiography
by Julius Evola

Journals published by Arktos:

The Initiate: Journal of Traditional Studies

Lightning Source UK Ltd.
Milton Keynes UK
UKOW04f0833100615

253247UK00004B/153/P